ESTABLISHING A
FORENSIC PSYCHIATRIC PRACTICE

A Practical Guide

ESTABLISHING A
FORENSIC PSYCHIATRIC PRACTICE

A Practical Guide

STEVEN H. BERGER, M.D.

W. W. Norton & Company
New York • London

Library of Congress Cataloging-in-Publication Data

Berger, Steven H.
    Establishing a forensic psychiatric practice : a practical guide /
Steven Berger
        p.   cm.
    Includes index
    ISBN 0-393-70252-9
    1. Forensic psychiatry — Handbooks, manuals, etc. I. Title.
RA1151.B35 1997
614'.1—dc21   97-10232   CIP

W.W. Norton & Company, Inc., 500 Fifth Avenue, New York, NY 10110
                    http://www.wwnorton.com
W.W. Norton & Company Ltd.,10 Coptic Street, London WC1A 1PU

1 2 3 4 5 6 7 8 9 0

To my loving, supportive wife

CONTENTS

Appendices

INTRODUCTION

When I began doing forensic psychiatry work in 1979, it presented a new, exciting challenge. Applying medical and psychiatric knowledge to legal questions is like putting a square peg in a round hole. It doesn't quite fit, but the system requires that it fit. So it is made to fit, even if awkwardly at times.

In forensic psychiatry, the psychiatrist does not determine how to make the peg fit. The attorney does that. The attorney is the strategist. The forensic psychiatrist is the gatherer and supplier of data. The attorney determines whether and how the data will be used. Thus, the practice of forensic psychiatry is like making a diagnosis, but not treating the patient. The forensic psychiatrist hands his diagnostic information over to the attorney, who then decides what will be done with it.

The system is not the medical system, in which the psychiatrist was trained. The system is the legal system, which seems to have more exceptions than rules. Whereas the highest priority in the medical system is health, in the legal system it is justice. Health is not viewed identically by all people, and justice isn't either. In the same way that illness seems unfair, justice often seems unfair.

Psychiatrists didn't ask to be drawn into legal matters. There are times when psychiatric testimony is required by the legal system. One example is the patient who, after years of long-term, stable medication treatment sustains a work-related posttraumatic stress disorder, caused by his witnessing a coworker fall 30 feet from a scaffold. The worker's compensation system denies benefits to the patient, contending that his longstanding psychiatric illness, not the employment-related incident, caused his current symptoms. The treating psychiatrist will likely be subpoenaed to testify as to his patient's condition before and after the work incident, and the cause of the present symptoms.

Another example is a hospital patient who withdraws his voluntary consent for treatment. The treating psychiatrist, and perhaps a consulting psychiatrist too, will be drawn into the patient's civil commitment process. Written reports and live testimony will be required of the psychiatrists.

Another example is a patient who seeks treatment for depression due to the shooting death of her husband. After a few weeks of treatment, the patient is arrested, accused of murdering her husband. The treating psychiatrist will likely be asked to testify in her defense. Or the treating psychiatrist might be asked to testify on behalf of the prosecution.

The last example is a patient being treated for anxiety disorder. The patient has been off work for four months due to his psychiatric illness. The patient's disability insurance company, or Social Security, asks for a report detailing the patient's abilities and limitations. Then the psychiatrist is deposed by the insurance company's attorney, or by the patient's attorney, in the legal struggle over the benefits eligibility question.

Some legal questions require psychiatric testimony, for example, when a prosecutor must prove intent. Psychiatrists who are drawn into the legal arena enjoy the challenge of fitting the square pegs into the round holes.

This book is a practical guide for psychiatrists entering the legal arena, either by choice or by force. It is a distillate of the lessons I have learned from my teachers, my books, and my experience. It is a collection of "nuts and bolts" information about how to do forensic psychiatry. And so, the book starts with a practical foundation: definitions of the more common terms used in forensic psychiatry. Next is an overview of how the duty of a forensic psychiatrist differs from the duty of a treating psychiatrist. Then the nuts and bolts are presented, including the way to establish a contract for the psychiatrist's services and how to review records, including medical, police, employment, school, and others. How to conduct a forensic examination is also discussed. Perhaps the most critical chapter is on writing reports, since the report is the vehicle by which the psychiatrist has the greatest impact on a forensic case.

The book then describes how to handle subpoenas, depositions, and trials. No guide to the legal arena would be complete without discussions of the ethical principles of forensic psychiatry and malpractice insurance, more accurately called professional liability insurance; these comprise chapters 10 and 11. The final chapter offers suggestions for advertising a forensic psychiatric practice. To round out the book, there are several appendices, which include board certification, forensic psychiatry organizations, suggested readings, and examples of forensic psychiatry reports.

Forensic psychiatry is a system of fitting medical square pegs into legal round holes. Colleagues are the best source of information on how this system really works. This book is a primer for my colleagues, a sharing of information with them.

One

DEFINITIONS

Affidavit A written statement by a witness that carries the same weight as sworn testimony.

Appeals court The court that determines whether the law was correctly applied to a trial. Only points of law are appealed. Points of fact are not appealed. Appeals courts are known by many different names, such as supreme court or district court of appeals.

Attorney work product The information gathered by an attorney. It includes verbal, written, and observed data. It includes all the media on which data is recorded, such as documents, videotapes, and computer memory disks. This is privileged information; its release cannot be forced.

Civil case A case in which a defendant is sued by a plaintiff for money or for injunctive relief (also known as tort case).

Client The client of the forensic psychiatrist is the attorney, insurance company, employer, or other party who retains the psychiatrist to serve as an expert witness on a case.

Criminal case A case in which a defendant is charged with a criminal act. A defendant found guilty is sentenced to jail or prison time, probation, a fine, or a number of hours of community service.

Deposition Sworn testimony given in a setting other than a courtroom, for example, the doctor's office or an attorney's office.

Discovery The gathering of information. Information can be discovered from people or from documents, videotapes, computer memory disks, etc. Our legal system has rules for discovery. Lawsuits have time limits for discovery of information that will be used in adjudicating a case. After the close of discovery, no additional information can be added for presentation to the factfinder at a trial. Some information is not discoverable, for example, an attorney is not allowed to discover the opposing attorney's work product.

Examinee The person who is evaluated by the forensic psychiatrist, the person about whom the expert witness testifies.

Expert witness A person who has special skill, knowledge, training, or experience not held by the common juror. The forensic psychiatrist is an expert witness. An expert witness is allowed to give opinion testimony within his field of expertise. An example of a question eliciting opinion testimony is, "In your opinion, doctor, is this defendant able to distinguish real voices from hallucinated voices?"

Fact witness A person who testifies as to facts, for example, what he saw or heard, where he last saw the defendant, or who handed her the smoking gun. Fact witnesses are generally not allowed to give opinions as testimony.

Factfinder The jury. In the absence of a jury, the judge.

Forensic psychiatry The subspecialty of psychiatry in which scientific and clinical expertise is applied to legal issues in legal contexts embracing civil, criminal, correctional, and legislative matters. (Treating patients in a correctional setting is often called forensic psychiatry, especially by physician recruiters or in other countries. This book is not about treating patients.)

Injunctive relief A court order to a party in a lawsuit to perform some act (for example, clean up the ground pollution or stop polluting the air).

Plaintiff The party who sues another party in a civil case.

Point of fact A determination by the factfinder of guilt or innocence in a criminal case or the winner in a civil case. Points of fact are disputed until the factfinder determines the facts.

Point of law The application of the law to a particular question in a trial. The judge determines the answers to such questions in the course of a trial, for example, whether a particular witness will be allowed to testify or whether a witness can be asked a particular question that might be prejudicial.

Prosecutor The attorney representing the people of the state (or municipality or federal government) in a criminal case.

Reasonable medical certainty Also known as reasonable medical probability. The degree of certainty with which a medical opinion is offered by an expert witness into evidence. This level of certainty is commonly said to be 51 percent, a bit more likely correct than incorrect; in some jurisdictions it is higher.

Subpoena An order to appear at a deposition or trial. A subpoena can be an order for a person to appear or to deliver medical records. Subpoenas are issued by attorneys or judges.

Trial court The court that determines guilt or innocence in a criminal case or the winner of a civil case. Trial courts are known by many different names, such as district court, circuit court, and traffic court. Each level of government has its own courts, such as city, county, state, and federal.

Two

THE DUTY OF THE FORENSIC PSYCHIATRIST

WHAT IS DUTY?

Duty is the obligation that the physician has to his* client. Most times, the forensic psychiatrist's client is the referring attorney in a case. In treating a patient, the physician's duty is to treat the patient in the same or similar way that other physicians would treat a similar patient in a similar situation; a forensic psychiatrist's duty is to fulfill the contractual obligation that he has to his client. These are very different duties.

The forensic psychiatrist's duty is not to treat the examinee. (In this book, forensic psychiatry does not refer to treating patients in correctional settings.) In fact, the forensic psychiatrist should *not* treat the examinee.

The forensic psychiatrist's duty is to review the records of the case, examine the examinee if appropriate, discuss the case with his client (usually the referring attorney), produce a report if requested by the referring attorney, advise the referring attorney as to his psychiatric questions regarding the case, and testify. The

*I have taken the liberty of using the masculine pronoun throughout the book; it is the one I am most comfortable using, having been taught in my early school days to use it to refer to both men and women.

testimony might be by affidavit, deposition, or testimony in open court. Testimony in a particular case might be by two or all three of these methods. These services are discussed in the next chapter.

To Whom does the Forensic Psychiatrist Have a Duty?

The forensic psychiatrist's duty is to his client (called the referring attorney in this book, so as not to be confused with a client patient whom one treats). The forensic psychiatrist's duty is not to the examinee, the court, or any other party. All communication about a case, both from the forensic psychiatrist and to the forensic psychiatrist, should go through the referring attorney. If the examinee or the court asks for a copy of the psychiatrist's report, a change in the time of the examination, or anything else, the answer should be channeled through the referring attorney. This is like a repair to a new car by a dealer, when the car is still under warranty. If the car needs a new battery, the buyer does not go to the car manufacturer or battery manufacturer. The buyer goes to the dealer, and the dealer goes to the manufacturer. The buyer has only one party through whom all dealings should go. The forensic psychiatrist has only one party, his referring attorney, through whom all dealings should be channeled.

The forensic psychiatrist has no duty to the examinee except to interact with the examinee respectfully. The forensic psychiatrist has no obligation to the examinee to answer questions, provide information, give a copy of his report, or anything else.

The only duty the forensic psychiatrist has to the court is to follow the court rules and behave respectfully. Attorneys are considered officers of the court, but witnesses and expert witnesses are not.

Dual Agency

Dual agency is owing a duty to two different parties. One example is an Army psychiatrist who owes a doctor-patient duty to his patient, and simultaneously owes a military security duty to the

Army. Sometimes these two duties conflict. Thus, if an Army psychiatrist's patient tells him that he has LSD in his footlocker, the psychiatrist may have to breach the confidentiality duty of his doctor-patient relationship in order to fulfill his duty to maintain the military security of the Army base. His duty to Army security requires him to report his patient's breach of security.

A more troubling situation is being both the treating psychiatrist of the patient and the forensic psychiatrist for the patient's attorney. The psychiatrist has a duty to his patient: to do what is best for the patient's health. But the psychiatrist also has a duty to the patient's attorney: to do what is in the patient's best legal interest. In this situation, the psychiatrist is the agent of the patient for treatment purposes and the agent of the attorney for forensic purposes. Sometimes these two duties conflict.

For example, a long-term patient commits a nonviolent crime. The patient's attorney asks the treating psychiatrist to also serve as the forensic psychiatry expert witness. The attorney wants the patient to plead guilty, which will bring a sentence of at least six months in jail. The patient wants to plead not guilty by reason of insanity in order to avoid jail and a criminal record.

In such a case, the psychiatrist cannot serve both masters. If the psychiatrist does as the patient wishes, and the case does not go as the patient hopes, then the patient is likely to be angry at the psychiatrist for the poor legal outcome. This will disrupt the therapeutic relationship between the psychiatrist and the patient, perhaps so severely that the psychiatrist will no longer be able to treat the patient. If the psychiatrist does as the attorney wishes, then the patient will likely be angry at the psychiatrist for that too.

In such a case, the psychiatrist is not free to make his own objective determination of whether the patient fulfills the criteria for legal insanity. The psychiatrist has the patient's needs pulling him in the direction of the patient's preference.

When a treatment case requires a forensic psychiatrist, it is advisable for the treating psychiatrist to maintain his treatment role and not to also become the expert witness for the legal case. He can offer fact testimony as the treating psychiatrist without offering opinion testimony on the question of legal sanity. The attorney can retain a different person to serve as the forensic psychiatrist to testify as to legal insanity. Of course, the patient will have to be evaluated by the second psychiatrist for that purpose.

The treating psychiatrist would be wise to discuss with the attorney the psychiatric facts of the case, with, of course, the patient's consent. If the facts are detrimental to the patient's defense, the attorney may prefer to keep the treating psychiatrist from testifying at all.

If the treating psychiatrist does testify, it would be advisable to discuss with his patient that he may be forced to reveal information that is detrimental or embarrassing to the patient. In that event, or in the event of an undesirable outcome at trial, the doctor-patient relationship may be fractured, perhaps irreparably. It is permissible for a treating psychiatrist, for the best interest of his patient, to refuse to testify in a legal matter. The treating psychiatrist can be forced to testify, however, as described in chapter 7.

Being an Advocate

An advocate is a person who argues for one particular side of a question. If a person argues that abortions should never be performed, then that person is an advocate for the pro-life position. If a forensic psychiatrist argues and "builds a case" supporting a conclusion, for example, that the examinee was emotionally harmed by her supervisor's sexual harassment, then the psychiatrist is advocating for that conclusion.

It is acceptable, sometimes desirable, for a forensic psychiatrist to advocate for a conclusion he has reached in his evaluation of a case. This is acceptable only if the advocated conclusion is reached after performing an impartial, objective evaluation. Advocating a viewpoint about a case prior to objectively evaluating the case is not acceptable for an ethical forensic psychiatrist. (Advocacy is further discussed in chapter 10, Ethics of Forensic Psychiatry.)

Hired Guns

A hired gun is an expert witness who testifies whatever his referring attorney wants him to testify. Hired guns are considered dishonorable and dishonest. A hired gun does not base his testimony on an objective evaluation. In contrast, an ethical forensic psychiatrist advocates his own objectively reached conclusion.

ONE-SIDEDNESS

One-sidedness is the practice of working only on one side of cases. A one-sided forensic psychiatrist works only on the defense side, only on the plaintiff's side, or only on the prosecutor's side of cases. One-sidedness is undesirable for a forensic psychiatrist because it suggests that he (1) is an advocate for one particular side of an issue, (2) performs evaluations that are less objective than they might be, or, even worse, (3) is a hired gun.

It is desirable for a forensic psychiatrist to work on the defense side of some cases and the other side of other cases. Such a distribution reinforces the principles of objectivity and impartiality in the evaluation of cases. A forensic psychiatrist is more credible if he is retained in cases on both sides of issues.

TYPES OF CASES

The variety of cases in which forensic psychiatrists are asked to participate is constantly expanding. Some questions fall under more than one category. The following are examples of the types of cases and questions asked.

1. General questions
   - Diagnostic evaluation: What is the psychiatric diagnosis of the examinee?
2. Personal injury cases (civil torts)
   - Liability evaluation: What caused the examinee's psychiatric disorder?
   - Damage evaluation: How much pain, suffering, humiliation, financial loss, loss of quality of life, etc., has the examinee sustained to this point, and how much such loss is expected in the future?

- Disability evaluation: What are the limitations in functioning caused by the psychiatric condition?
- Sexual harassment evaluation: Was the plaintiff sexually harassed by the employer?

3. Criminal cases
   - Insanity evaluation: Did the defendant fulfill the criteria for legal insanity at the time of the offense?
   - Presentencing evaluation: What sentence for the guilty party would fulfill the needs of the criminal justice system?
   - Prerelease evaluation: What monitoring is needed to fulfill the safety needs of the community in releasing the offender?
   - Juvenile waiver evaluation: Should the juvenile be tried as an adult?

4. Competency evaluations
   - In criminal cases, competence to stand trial, plead, be sentenced, be executed, proceed (with the next step in the adjudication process).
   - In civil cases, competence to sign a will, consent to medical treatment, testify, get married, sign a contract, etc.
   - Undue influence: Was the deceased the subject of undue influence when he signed the will?

5. Probate questions
   - Competence to parent: Is the adult competent to provide parenting?
   - Best interest of a child evaluation: Does this child have needs that cannot be filled by the parent?
   - Visitation evaluation: Will contact with the parent be harmful to the child?

6. Malpractice cases
   - Standard of care evaluation: Did the physician's treatment fulfill the standard of care?

7. Disability evaluations
   - Americans with Disabilities Act (ADA) evaluation: Does the plaintiff fulfill the ADA definition of a disabled person? What accommodation is needed for the disabled plaintiff to be able to perform the essential functions of his employment?
   - Fitness for duty evaluation: Is the examinee now able to perform his usual employment duties?

8. Discrimination evaluations: Is the plaintiff a member of a protected group and was he subjected to discrimination due to being a member of that protected group?
9. Dangerousness evaluations: Is the person a danger to himself or others?
10. Civil commitment evaluations: Does the person fulfill the criteria for civil commitment?
11. Insurance coverage evaluations: Does the plaintiff fulfill the insurance policy's definition of a person with a preexisting condition?

Withdrawing from a Case

There are times when it is appropriate for a forensic psychiatrist to withdraw from a case. One example is when the retaining attorney expects the forensic psychiatrist to sacrifice objectivity in his evaluation, conclusions, or testimony. Another is when dishonesty, or any other unethical practice, is expected of the forensic psychiatrist. Another is when any aspect of the contract for services is broken, such as when the retaining attorney fails to pay the psychiatrist's bill. The forensic psychiatrist should also withdraw from a case when he is unable, for whatever reason, to perform the contracted service.

Keeping a List of Testimonies

In federal cases, an attorney is permitted to require an expert witness to produce a list of all cases in which he has testified during the past three years. Such a list is also requested, on occasion, in other cases. It is prudent for a forensic psychiatrist to maintain this list of cases. For each case, the list should include:

1. Name of case
2. Docket number
3. Court of jurisdiction

4. Date of testimony
5. Place where testimony was rendered
6. Retaining attorney's name, address, phone, and fax numbers
7. Retaining attorney's side (plaintiff, defense, prosecution)
8. Nature of case
   • Criminal or civil
   • One- or two-word description of the case (larceny, murder, sexual harassment, workers' compensation, etc.)

KEEPING A CURRENT CURRICULUM VITAE

Referral sources commonly request a curriculum vitae (CV) from a forensic psychiatrist. A forensic psychiatrist should always keep a few copies of his CV on hand. It is also wise to update it every two to six months, so that it is never more than half a year old.

In a deposition, it is common for an attorney to simply have the expert witness's CV typed into the text, or attached to the deposition transcript. That way, time is saved: The attorney does not have to ask the expert to verbalize all the items on the CV.

A complete CV lists all of the credentials and relevant history of the individual. Because a forensic psychiatrist is a physician first, psychiatrist second, and forensic psychiatrist third, the CV should list the elements of each status. A forensic psychiatrist's CV should include:

1. Name
2. Professional address, phone and fax numbers, and e-mail address
3. Previous professional addresses and dates
4. Educational history starting with college, including residencies and fellowships, dates, and degrees
5. Professional society memberships, offices held, and dates
6. Professional employment and positions, including addresses and dates
7. States in which a medical license has been held, license number, and dates
8. Board certifications and dates obtained and renewed

9. Academic appointments held, addresses, and dates
10. Professional administrative positions held, addresses, and dates
11. Consultant positions held, addresses, and dates
12. Hospital staff memberships, addresses, and dates
13. Editorial positions in medical publications, and dates
14. Professional presentations, name of the organizations, places, and dates
15. Community education presentations, places, and dates
16. Other relevant data
17. Publications (bibliography)

HANDOUTS

In depositions, expert witnesses are sometimes asked to produce copies of things listed in one's CV. Examples of requested items might be copies of papers published, media interviews, programs presented, or a list of previous testimonies. It is much easier for an expert witness to comply with such requests if he keeps copies of such items handy.

If a deposition takes place in a location other than the forensic psychiatrist's office and such documents are requested, the psychiatrist can offer to send them to the retaining attorney the next day.

Three

Establishing a Service Agreement

Initial Contact

A case starts with a phone call to the forensic psychiatrist. The call comes from the psychiatrist's client, the referring attorney. The forensic psychiatrist's client is an attorney, an insurance company, an employer, or a similar party. Sometimes the contact is in writing.

In the first contact, the referring attorney will describe the nature of the case and the parties involved. If the psychiatrist has any conflict of interest, vested interest, or prior involvement in the case, it should be mentioned at this time, and the conversation will likely stop, with no further information exchanged and no contract for the psychiatrist's services.

If the psychiatrist has a prejudice in the issue at hand, then it is prudent for the psychiatrist to mention it at this time. The prejudice may be advantageous, disadvantageous, or irrelevant to the psychiatrist's involvement in the case. An example is a case of a woman who is depressed because she was coerced by her boyfriend to have an abortion. If the psychiatrist has a bias on the question of abortion, it should be revealed to the referring attorney at this point.

The referring attorney will ask the psychiatrist if he is willing to be a consultant or an expert witness in the case. If such an agreement is made, then the financial and logistical arrangements are discussed. After such arrangements are verbally agreed upon, then the service agreement should be signed by the attorney. The service agreement is discussed below.

A referring attorney may ask, as part of these initial agreements, if the psychiatrist will testify a particular way on the question at hand. It is unwise for the psychiatrist to say yes or no at that point. It is better to say that, if the data supports such a conclusion, then yes, such testimony would be rendered.

Occasionally, an examinee will call to arrange for the psychiatrist's involvement. It is generally advisable to recommend that the examinee have his attorney call the psychiatrist. Some forensic psychiatrists will make an exception in the case of a wealthy examinee who is willing to deposit a large retainer fee. Still, contracting for forensic services directly with the person who is a party to the issue is not recommended because (1) the expert witness is an agent of the attorney and not the litigant, (2) the psychiatrist's roles of treater and forensic expert become easily confused in such an arrangement, and (3) it is difficult to portray objectivity in such an arrangement.

Written Correspondence

A forensic psychiatrist should wait to begin work on a case until the signed written correspondence is received. Faxed documents with signatures are acceptable, but they should be followed up with hard copies.

The written correspondence should include the provisions of the agreement between the retaining attorney and the psychiatrist. This can be in the form of a letter or a contract. It should include the name of the case, the fee arrangement, and the questions the psychiatrist is being asked to address. The questions should be as specific and direct as possible. It is much easier and more helpful to address "Is George Gilbert psychiatrically able to resume his usual work duties at the ABC Corporation?" than "Please comment on George's ability to work." The number of questions may be small or large.

If an examination is to occur, then the written correspondence should state the time and place of the examination. Getting the examinee to the examination is the responsibility of the retaining attorney, not the psychiatrist. If the examinee does not show up for the examination, or is late, then the written correspondence can be used to show that the psychiatrist did not fail to provide his contracted services. In such a case, the retaining attorney is the one who failed to have the examinee present. The retaining attorney is then responsible for paying for the psychiatrist's unused time. Obviously, to make such a claim, the psychiatrist must be present and available at the appointed time and place, and he must have written confirmation from the retaining attorney as to the predetermined time and place.

Service Agreement

The service agreement* consists of two parts: an introductory cover letter and a list of services. At the top of each page, the referring attorney's name and address and the name of the case are written. The letter begins on letterhead stationery:

```
Attorney Alan Addington
123 Main Street
Detroit, Michigan 12345-6789

Re: Billy Baker vs. General Motors Corporation

Dear Mr. Addington:
```

---

*The suggested service agreement is printed here as public domain. It may be copied, modified, and used by readers at will. It is adapted from the documents used by my teachers, Emanual Tanay, M.D., of Detroit, and Phillip Resnick, M.D., of Cleveland.

The first paragraph is an introduction:

> Thank you for referring your questions regard-
> ing the above case to me for forensic psychi-
> atric evaluation. I will be glad to offer my
> professional services regarding this case.

The next paragraph explains that insurance companies (as well as governmental agencies, some employers, and some favored referral sources) are not required to make advance payments. "Normal" referring attorneys and other referral sources are required to, however.

> Before I reserve time for this case, I ask
> that you send payment for the time that is
> expected to be devoted to this case. (Insur-
> ance companies and governmental units may pay
> after services are rendered, in response to my
> monthly bill, but only if payment is guaran-
> teed by letter, or by the attached agreement,
> signed by an employee or attorney who has
> authority to enter into such an agreement.)
> This amount is advance payment to be applied
> to my final billing. In the event that time
> devoted to this case exceeds that covered by
> the advance deposit amount, I will bill you
> for the additional time. Payment will be
> expected promptly upon such additional
> billing. It is not my intention to distrust
> you; it is my intention to be compensated for
> my time.

If a letter guaranteeing payment is used instead of a service agreement, then the letter should contain all the elements of the service agreement, including the explicit fee agreement.

The next paragraph lists the services that are to be paid at the hourly rate. Basically, all time spent on a case is to be paid by the retaining attorney (or other retaining party). Waiting time includes time spent waiting for an examinee to arrive for his scheduled examination, as well as time spent waiting to testify in court, etc.

```
My fee is $XXX.XX per 60 minutes for reviewing
records, performing examinations, preparing
reports, conferring with attorneys, travel
time, testifying time, waiting time, or time
spent in any other way on this specific case.
Depositions are scheduled for a minimum of two
hours. Court appearances are scheduled for
either four hours or eight hours per day.
```

The next paragraph documents the recommendation that all records should be reviewed by the forensic psychiatrist. Referring attorneys may send only some of the records, in order to reduce the number of hours the psychiatrist spends on the case. However, that should be the referring party's decision, not the psychiatrist's. Which materials are reviewed by the expert witness is a question of legal strategy, not a question of medical judgment.

```
I recommend that you have me review all rele-
vant medical reports, depositions, investiga-
tion reports, photographs, and other helpful
information prior to my examination of the
subject. In order to make the most efficient
use of my time, I suggest that you send all
such records at least two weeks prior to the
scheduled examination of the examinee.
```

All materials sent for the psychiatrist's review should indeed be reviewed. Sometimes psychiatrists use readers, the way attorneys use paralegal assistants, to read records for them, and pick out the relevant parts. The psychiatrist is held responsible by the referring party for reviewing all of the documents sent.

In estimating the cost of reviewing records, two hours per inch (measured in inches of height of the pile of pages) is a helpful guideline. Condensed depositions take up to 12 hours per inch, depending on how condensed they are.

The next paragraph documents the fee arrangements. The more explicit, the better. In the model described here, a typical examination consists of two appointments of 2¼ hours each, one week apart. Common practice is to charge for cancelled time, if the time cannot be filled with another paid activity, such as reading the file on another forensic case, or treating patients. Such a charge is made for cancellations less than two weeks in advance for reserved blocks of time greater than 2¼ hours. Such a charge is made for cancellations less than 48 hours in advance for reserved blocks of time of 2¼ hours or less.

```
Payment is expected two weeks before any
appointment. If payment is not received when
expected, the appointment will be automati-
cally cancelled. Full payment will be expected
for appointments not kept, or for appointments
not cancelled 48 hours in advance. A charge
may be made for deposition time, court time,
or blocks of time longer than 2¼ hours, not
cancelled two weeks in advance.
```

If the 4½-hour examination is split into two parts, and the examinee fails to show up for the first appointment, then the referring attorney can cancel the second appointment and reschedule. That way, the referring attorney has to pay for only 2¼ hours of unused time instead of 4½ hours.

The person signing a letter guaranteeing payment or the service agreement must be a person who has the authority to enter into such contracts: for insurance companies, that is commonly a claims adjuster; for law firms, an attorney or a paralegal assistant; for a business, an officer of the corporation, personnel department employee, or owner of the business; for a prosecutor, the prosecutor or the county treasurer; for a court, a judge or a magistrate. A judge, instead of a letter, will often issue a court order for the government to pay the psychiatrist's bill, which is acceptable.

The following is the concluding paragraph and signature of the cover letter portion of the service agreement:

```
Please sign the enclosed original agreement
for my services regarding this case and return
it along with the required advance payment.
Thank you for allowing me to contract with you
in this way. Please call any time you have
questions or further information.

Sincerely yours,


Frederick F. Forensic, M.D.
Diplomate, American Board of Psychiatry and
Neurology, with  Added Qualifications in
Forensic Psychiatry
```

The specifications portion of the service agreement starts on the next page. It should be on another page of letterhead stationery. At the top of the page is typed the retaining attorney's name and address, and the name of the case:

```
Attorney Alan Addington
123 Main Street
Detroit, Michigan 12345-6789

Re: Billy Baker vs. General Motors Corporation

            SERVICE AGREEMENT

As per your request, time has been reserved
regarding the above case for:
```

_____ Review of records, estimated _____ hours.
_____ Examination of examinee scheduled for

_____
_____

_____ Preparation of report, estimated _____
        hours.
_____ Deposition (two hours minimum time
        reserved) scheduled at my office for

_____
_____

_____ Court appearance on _____
_____ Conference with attorney by phone or in
        person, travel time, other time devoted
        specifically to this case, estimated
        _____ hours.

The blanks are checked and filled in by the psychiatrist. At the time of the initial agreement, it is acceptable to list only some services and fees, anticipating that more will be added if the case progresses.

The required advance payment is then filled in. For insurance companies and other trusted clients, "per monthly billing" can be written instead of a dollar amount.

Please sign below, indicating your acceptance of this agreement and the contractual provisions contained in the accompanying cover letter. Please keep a photocopy of this agreement for your records, and return these two pages to me with your advance payment of $_____.

The concluding paragraph and signature follow:

```
Thank you for allowing me to arrange for the
provision of my services to you in this way.

Sincerely yours,


Frederick F. Forensic, M.D.
Diplomate, American Board of Psychiatry and Neu-
rology, with Added Qualifications in Forensic
Psychiatry

Tax ID#: 12-3456789
```

The tax identification number of the recipient of the payment (Dr. Forensic, Dr. Forensic's P.C., Detroit Psychiatric Service, or whatever is the business entity receiving the payment) is listed below the psychiatrist's signature. This number is required by clients so they can tax deduct the payments as business expenses.

Last is the blank for the referring attorney, or authorized person, to sign the agreement:

```
Contract accepted by:
_____

Date:_____
```

If the cover letter and specifications sections of the service agreement require more than one page each, then it is wise to put the name of the case at the top of each page. This is helpful in case the pages become separated.

It is prudent to wait until the signed specifications page is received, along with any required advance payment, before the psychiatrist begins spending time on a case.

Fees are commonly quoted per hour. Note that it is easier to have a fee that is divisible by 10. Attorneys commonly bill by the quarter- or tenth-hour. It is also reasonable for forensic psychiatrists to do so. Psychiatrists whose fees are divisible by 4 or 10 avoid having to bill for less than a whole dollar amount. For example, one tenth of $230 per hour is $23.00, whereas one tenth of $225 per hour is $22.50.

PREVENTIVE CONTRACTING

Preventive contracting is the contracting with an expert only for the purpose of preventing another party from contracting with the expert for the same case.

At the moment that the expert witness is given any information about a case by a retaining attorney, or a potentially retaining attorney, the expert becomes a member of that attorney's team. The expert then has knowledge about the case, the attorney's strategy, the attorney's thoughts, or some aspect of the attorney's information base. Because of this knowledge, the expert may, ethically, have contact with the other parties in a lawsuit only when the contact is controlled by the retaining attorney. This is because the knowledge held by the expert is attorney work product.

Attorney work product is not discoverable. Discoverable information is information to which others are allowed access. Attorney work product is the work, research, writings, thinking, and communications of the attorney. The opposing side in a litigation is not allowed to discover anything that is Attorney A's work product without Attorney A's consent. The opposing side is allowed to gather information that might be the identical information as Attorney A's work product, but such information must be gathered from some source other than Attorney A.

For example, Alan Harasser's attorney, Attorney Don Defense, has his assistant, Ivan Investigator, interview a witness, Mrs. Eyes. Mr. Investigator learns that Mrs. Eyes saw Alan Harasser harassing Mrs. Victim. Mrs. Victim's attorney, Paul Plaintiff, may gather the same information from Mrs. Eyes, but he may not gather that information from Ivan Investigator. The knowledge held by Ivan Investigator is Attorney Don Defense's work product, and is therefore not discoverable by Attorney Paul Plaintiff.

The expert witness has the same role as Ivan Investigator. The expert gathers or processes information for the attorney, as a member of the attorney's team. Once he gains information from the attorney's team, he becomes a team member. He is then unavailable to the other side, except as controlled by the attorney who is the captain of his team.

Preventive contracting is a way of keeping the other side from using a particular expert. For example, if Professor Sleepless is the world's expert on mania, and Attorney Plaintiff knows that Professor Sleepless will give testimony detrimental to his client's claim, then Attorney Plaintiff might, as a strategic move, discuss the case with Professor Sleepless, asking if the professor would be interested in serving as an expert witness for the plaintiff. No matter how Professor Sleepless replies, he has become "tainted" because Attorney Plaintiff has given him information about the plaintiff's side of the case. After the information is received by the professor, he is no longer able, ethically or legally, to be an expert witness for the defense side in the lawsuit.

Commonly, psychiatrists do not take steps to avoid becoming tainted by preventive contracting because it happens so infrequently to most experts. Preventive contracting is more likely to be used with highly prestigious or widely known experts.

The way to reduce the risk of becoming a victim of preventive contracting is for the expert to get a retainer fee from the attorney prior to receiving any information about the case. Additional ways to reduce the risk are to get a signed service agreement, a few hours worth of documents to read, or a guarantee of a minimum payment before receiving any information about the case. Most experts do not take such steps for fear of alienating the sincere attorney and losing the opportunity to participate in the case.

Four

REVIEWING RECORDS

WHAT TO REVIEW

As discussed in chapter 3, the service agreement cover letter should recommend that the retaining attorney send to the expert all relevant medical reports, deposition transcripts, investigation reports, photographs, and other helpful information. The more information the expert has, the better able he is to evaluate the case. More information will lend greater validity to his thoughts and opinions about the case.

An expert should review all the material he has received. If an expert is asked during testimony if he reviewed a document that he was sent and he did not, but is offering testimony on the case, the expert appears to have done a less than complete job of reviewing the case.

HOW TO ORGANIZE RECORDS

Records come in all shapes and sizes. Some records are loose pages, some are bound documents, such as deposition transcripts, and some are hospital records with pages in various sections.

Records often arrive in stages. Noting when records are received is judicious. Sometimes one must determine in retrospect whether he reviewed a particular document before or after another event occurred. For example, an expert might be asked in a deposition if he read a particular document before or after he wrote his July 1, 1996, report.

Some documents are numbered by the attorney's office before they are sent to the expert. Commonly, those are six-digit numbers stamped on a corner of each page. Some documents, such as deposition transcripts, have text numbered pages.

An easy way to keep the documents in order for later reference is to number them in a pattern that is distinct from any other numbering pattern already on the pages. For example, if the second packet of documents contains a three-page letter, a hospital record, and two deposition transcripts, the pages in that packet can be numbered by the expert in this way: BA 1-3 for the letter, BB 1-150 for the hospital record, and BC 1-80 and BD 1-125 for the two depositions. The first letter, B, indicates that this document was in the second packet of documents received. The second letter refers to the particular document in the second packet, and the number refers to the page number of the document. The expert must number the pages of the hospital record. The pages of the letter and depositions will already be numbered, so the expert need only add the letters at the beginning of numbers.

It is not necessary to number every page, unless the pages are going to be separated and not kept in order. Only the pages that have significance need to be numbered. The first page of each document should be numbered in order to identify the document.

It is not necessary to keep a table of contents or list of documents received, although that might be helpful. Some experts put records in binders of various sorts, complete with a table of contents and index. Some experts simply keep the collection of documents in a loose file folder, similar to common office charts of patients.

There is no standard order for organizing records. An expert might find it most convenient to organize records alphabetically, chronologically, by type of document, in the order in which they were received or reviewed, or in any other pattern.

How to Take Notes when Reviewing Records

Taking notes when reviewing records is important, both for remembering and cross-referencing data. Notes should include the data, or references to data, that the expert finds relevant to the questions he is asked to address. Notes should include the page number, so the original reference can be easily found. It is helpful if notes also include dates of significant events (keeping a time line is helpful) and the spelling of unusual words or names. The spelling notes are handy when the expert writes a report. The spelling words can be listed along the right-hand border of the first page of notes, in quasi-alphabetical order, so that they can be easily found.

It is helpful to start the notes of a case with the name of the case, names of the attorneys from both sides, and the name of the first document being reviewed. Then the first thing written in a particular notation should be the page on which the data is found. The numbering system detailed above is handy for this purpose. Notes can be abbreviated or spelled out, in whatever system is easiest for the expert.

If more than one page of notes is written, then numbering the pages of notes and putting the name of the case on each page is also helpful.

Where to Write Notes

Writing notes on the records being reviewed is not a good idea. The opposing attorney is allowed to ask for copies of all the documents reviewed by the expert and to discover all of the data on which the expert is basing his opinion. If the expert makes any notes, marks, highlights, or underlines on the records he reviews, the opposing attorney will see them. The retaining attorney or the expert may prefer to avoid the opposing attorney's having access to such notations.

The notes kept by the expert, as described above, are attorney work product. They are not discoverable in some jurisdictions.

Thus, it is wise for the expert to keep notes on his own notepaper, and not on the records themselves.

KEEPING TRACK OF READING TIME

For billing purposes, the expert must keep track of the amount of time he spends reviewing records. One way is to include in his notes the starting and ending time of his reading. Another way is to use a stopwatch, which may sound compulsive, but allows for the clock to be stopped if the phone rings or if other interruptions occur.

Attorneys commonly bill by the tenth-hour, in 6-minute blocks. The number of hours spent reading, to the first decimal place, can be written in the expert's notes so that he can later bill for his time: Less than 3 minutes does not count; between 3 and 9 minutes is 0.1 hour; between 9 and 15 minutes is 0.2 hours; between 57 and 63 minutes is 1.0 hour.

Five

CONDUCTING THE FORENSIC EXAMINATION

WHEN

The attorney who contracts with the psychiatric expert witness will arrange the time, and usually the place, for the psychiatrist to examine the examinee. Then the attorney will notify the examinee. If the examinee is not the client of the retaining attorney, then the retaining attorney will notify the examinee's attorney, who will then notify the examinee.

There are several reasons why the attorney, and not the psychiatrist, notifies the examinee of the time and place of the examination. One reason is that the psychiatrist's involvement with the examinee should be limited to the examination. There should be no interaction between the psychiatrist and the examinee regarding the arranging of the appointment time and place, transportation, lunch, etc. Such interactions can interfere with the psychiatrist's objectivity, and should therefore be avoided.

If a five-hour examination goes over the normal lunch time, it is appropriate to take a break for lunch. Recommending a restaurant to an examinee seems simple and polite. But if the examinee then tells the psychiatrist that the restaurant was horrible and the psychiatrist must have dead taste buds, then the psychiatrist may have some feelings about the examinee after lunch that he didn't have before lunch. Such feelings on the part of the examiner can influence his objectivity.

Another reason regards fees. If the examinee arrives late for the examination appointment or does not show up at all, the psychiatrist should bill the retaining attorney for the time reserved, just as if the examination were conducted. Time is time, whether it is used or not. If the examinee claims that he was tardy or absent because he was told a different time, date, or place, then it is the attorney's or the examinee's error, not the psychiatrist's. If the psychiatrist had been responsible for arranging the time and place, then the attorney could reasonably say that the psychiatrist was responsible for the unused time because the miscommunication must have been the psychiatrist's fault. In such a case, the retaining attorney could reasonably refuse to pay for the unused time.

The third reason regards the legalities of discovery. If the attorney is the one responsible for arranging the time and place, then any delays in the examination are his responsibility. The attorney is responsible for seeing that all examinations occur within the proper discovery period. The psychiatrist should avoid taking on this responsibility for meeting legal deadlines.

Another reason regards access to the examinee. If the examinee is in jail, for example, the psychiatrist will have a much easier time gaining access to the examinee if the attorney has made arrangements with the jail ahead of time. Attorneys have a much easier time making such arrangements than psychiatrists do.

One special situation regarding timing deserves mention here. A forensic examination should not be conducted on a detainee (a person who has been arrested) until after the detainee has conferred with his attorney. Examining a detainee prior to his conferring with his attorney is considered unethical. Also, any information so gathered may be unacceptable to the courts. However, a psychiatric examination for the purpose of treatment, with appropriate consent, is permissible prior to a detainee's conferring with his attorney.

WHERE

The most common location in which the examination takes place is the psychiatrist's office. Other places might be the retaining attorney's office, the opposing attorney's office, or a correctional facility.

If the examination occurs in a city other than the attorneys' cities, the examination might occur at the borrowed office of another attorney, the borrowed office of another physician, some other sort of office, a hospital conference room, a hotel conference room, a jail conference room, or a jail cell. In unusual circumstances, an examination might occur in a hospital room, the examinee's home, or other places. Using a hotel room, or a bedroom of any sort, is unwise because of the sexual implications of such a setting.

The examination room should be private. The information that the psychiatrist gathers during an examination is attorney work product. The attorney has the right to determine who receives the information gathered by the psychiatrist. Thus, the examination space should not be within the hearing range of others.

The examination room should be comfortable, furnished appropriate to the situation. A forensic evaluation, like an evaluation for treatment purposes, should be conducted under optimal circumstances when possible. This means a quiet room free of distractions. Telephone calls should be held, except for urgent calls that should not wait for a break in the examination. The setting should be as professional as the situation will allow.

HOW

The forensic psychiatric examination is conducted in basically the same manner as a standard psychiatric examination for diagnostic purposes: The psychiatrist asks questions and the examinee answers.

Medical ethics require that the psychiatrist provide competent medical service, with compassion and respect for human dignity.

(See chapter 10 for further discussion of ethics.) This ethical mandate also applies to forensic evaluations. Thus, the psychiatrist is obligated to avoid badgering, insulting, humiliating, or treating examinees disrespectfully in any other way. Respect also includes being prompt and avoiding keeping examinees waiting an unreasonable amount of time in the waiting room. Respect mandates appropriate bathroom breaks, lunch breaks, cigarette breaks for smokers, water, and such amenities that psychiatrists commonly allow patients.

The ethical requirement for competent medical service also means that a forensic psychiatrist should not attempt to perform an examination that he is not qualified to conduct. For example, if an examination is conducted in Spanish and the psychiatrist has only a limited ability to converse in Spanish, then an interpreter or a Spanish-speaking examiner should be used. Another example is examining children in a child custody evaluation or sexual abuse case when the psychiatrist has no training on how to conduct such examinations.

The questions the psychiatrist asks the examinee can include any and all areas of inquiry. A complete forensic examination includes all the questions asked in a routine diagnostic evaluation, including current psychiatric symptoms and treatments, past psychiatric symptoms and treatments, general medical history and treatments, and mental status examination. Questions regarding the legal claim at hand, of course, are a focus of the examination.

It is fair to ask leading questions (questions in which the answer is suggested in the question) and even trick questions, as long as the examiner remains objective in his interpretation of the information gathered. It is also fair to ask stressful and painful questions as long as the ethical requirements for compassion and respect for human dignity are fulfilled.

CONSENT

Consent is required for any medical intervention, including forensic psychiatric examinations. Medical examination or treatment without consent is considered to be assault and battery—a criminal offense.

An examinee is free to refuse consent for a forensic examination. If the examinee refuses to give consent to be examined, then the examination should not be conducted. The refusal should be reported to the retaining attorney. The retaining attorney then handles the refusal according to the requirements of the legal system.

Consent by an examinee's attorney is acceptable. Consent by a legal guardian or by the parent of a minor child is also acceptable. Of course, a court order for an examination is an acceptable substitute for consent.

One instance in which consent is not needed for a forensic examination is in the case of civil commitment. A forensic psychiatrist may conduct an examination without the examinee's consent for the purpose of determining whether the examinee fulfills the state's criteria for civil commitment.

The consent form* should be on letterhead stationery to maintain the medical tone of the evaluation. Numbering the paragraphs is helpful as a reference, if the examinee has questions about a particular paragraph. The form starts with the examinee's name:

```
1. I,_____,
   agree to be psychiatrically examined by
   Frederick F. Forensic, M.D.
```

The next paragraph lists the attorney (or other parties) who will receive the information gathered by the psychiatrist:

*The consent form detailed here is offered as public domain. It may be copied, modified, and used by readers at will. It is adapted from the documents used by my teachers, Emanuel Tanay, M.D., of Detroit, Michigan, and Phillip Resnick, M.D., of Cleveland, Ohio.

2. I agree to Dr. Forensic's releasing his
   report of his findings to:

   _____

   _____

The next paragraph is the usual release from liability clause:

3. I hereby release Dr. Forensic from any claim
   or liability resulting from the releasing of
   his report as described above, and from his
   releasing information about me in any trial
   or deposition.

The next paragraph regards specific consent to record the examination:

4. I agree to Dr. Forensic's audiorecording and
   videorecording his examination of me. I
   understand that any such recordings are considered medical records.

The next section is for the examinee's signature:

   Signed: _____

   Date: _____

A copy of the consent form should be given to the examinee.

Sometimes an examinee will give verbal consent but not written consent. This is acceptable. If the examination is audiotaped or videotaped from the time the examinee walks into the examining room, then the verbal consent is documented on tape, even if it is not documented on paper.

Sometimes an examinee will refuse to give consent until he talks to his attorney. This can be handled by allowing the examinee to phone his attorney. Privacy should be offered for the phone call. This can be done by offering the examinee the use of a phone in an unoccupied office or by allowing the examinee to leave and use a public phone.

Others Present During the Examination

It is preferable to conduct an examination with only the examinee present. However, in some circumstances, it *is* permissible to have others present. For example, a guest may be allowed to be present to alleviate the fear of the examinee. If the examinee is too afraid of the process, the examiner, the setting, the separation from trusted others, or for any other reason, the examiner may choose to have another person accompany the examinee. This commonly occurs, for example, with a child, a mentally retarded or geriatric examinee, or an examinee who has been traumatized and is afraid to be separated from a trusted companion.

Another reason for a guest to be present is to enhance the information that can be gathered. Examples are (1) the use of an interpreter if the examination is conducted in a language that is difficult for the examinee, (2) the presence of a companion when examining a mentally retarded person with limited language skills, or (3) the presence of a caretaker when examining a brain injured person with verbal aphasia.

Other situations involving guests include when the attorney for the examinee insists on being present for the examination or when a detainee is not allowed to be left without a police or corrections officer present. There are some circumstances in which an examinee is by statute allowed to bring a guest. In Michigan, for example, a workers' compensation claimant is allowed to bring his own physician to a medical examination arranged by the workers' compensation insurance company.

In situations where guests demand, or are required, to be present, a one-way-mirror room may fulfill the needs of all the parties. If the examination can be conducted with the guests viewing the process from the dark side of the mirror, then the examination can proceed without contamination from the observers. The one-way-mirror room can even be used without sound, so that the observers can see, but not hear, the examination process. This works especially well when the observer is a corrections officer.

If a one-way-mirror room is not available, guests should sit out of view of the examinee, for example, behind the examinee or off to the side. The purpose is to avoid coaching or cuing of the examinee by the guest. Coaching or cuing can be done verbally, with facial expressions, or with body language. If a guest does coach or cue, he can be asked to leave. If the examinee refuses to be examined alone or the guest refuses to leave, then the examination can be stopped. The retaining attorney should then be called and told why the examination could not proceed.

When guests assist in the communication process, there is significant risk of contamination of the information gathered. This contamination is to be considered in the examiner's judgment regarding the validity of the information gathered.

The Uncooperative Examinee

An examinee can be uncooperative by being tardy or absent, sarcastic and smart-mouthed, mute, disruptive, or by being resistant and uncooperative in answering questions.

The examiner can expect cooperation from the examinee in the same way that the examinee can expect to be treated respectfully by the examiner. If the examinee is being uncooperative in any way, it is prudent for the examiner to ask him to cooperate, even to the point of explaining that the examination will have to be rescheduled, perhaps with a different venue, if he remains uncooperative. If the examinee still does not cooperate, then the examination can be stopped. The referring attorney should then be called and told about the situation. It will then be up to him to handle the situation and reschedule the examination. An example solution is for the examination to be rescheduled with both attorneys present during the examination.

As mentioned earlier, an examinee is tardy or absent for a scheduled appointment, the examiner should charge for the time reserved.

THE UNCOOPERATIVE ATTORNEY

A retaining attorney can be uncooperative by failing to communicate, communicating in a confusing or ineffective manner, making unreasonable demands, making unclear requests, or by failing to pay the psychiatrist's bill.

It is reasonable to inform the retaining attorney of the needs of the forensic expert, and that the expert cannot continue to work on the case without the attorney's cooperation. If cooperation does not then occur, it is appropriate for the expert to withdraw from the case, with written notice to the attorney.

The attorney on the other side can be uncooperative by interfering with the examination of the examinee. The attorney can be disruptive during the examination, for example, he can be argumentative, coach and cue the examinee, refuse to allow the examination to proceed unless some demand of his is fulfilled, or advise his client to do or not do things, including answer questions.

When this occurs, the examination can be stopped for a break or it can be terminated. When stopped, the retaining attorney should be called and given a report about the situation. The examiner can then decide with the retaining attorney whether to proceed with the examination, and under what circumstances. The retaining attorney can take the same steps that are used to deal with an uncooperative examinee.

INTERRUPTIONS AND BREAKS

Taking breaks during an examination is acceptable. In the same way that courts take breaks about every two hours for bathroom, cigarette, and telephone use, such breaks during forensic examinations are advisable.

During breaks, the examinee should be given access to a bathroom. If the examinee smokes, he should be directed to a smoking area, if practical under the circumstances. Meanwhile, the examiner may check messages, make phone calls, and attend to similar matters. An appropriate amount of time for a break is 5–10 minutes. An appropriate amount of time for a lunch break is 60–90 minutes. Telling the examinee the time that the examination will resume is appropriate, otherwise the examinee will be the one to decide when the examination resumes.

Interruptions during a forensic examination should be treated similar to interruptions during a psychotherapy session. They are unwelcome and they interrupt the process. Interruptions should be limited to urgencies that cannot wait until the next break.

If a distraction occurs that interferes with the examination process, such as a loud garbage truck emptying a dumpster, a break should be taken until the distraction is resolved.

RECORDING OF EXAMINATIONS

Recording forensic examinations does not appear to be the standard of practice. There are, however, many advantages to the audio- or videorecording of forensic examinations. The most obvious is documentation. If, at any point, anyone raises a question as to what was said or not said, done or not done, or whether an inflection of voice was present or not, a recording can answer the question. Even if the examiner is the only one with a question, he can review the recording to double-check his recollection.

A recording reassures the examinee that the examiner is unlikely to misinterpret or incorrectly report the things the examinee says. With every word documented, the examinee can answer questions with an expectation that his answers will be accurately reported by the examiner.

If a claim is made that the examiner was harsh, cruel, unfair, demanding, pressuring, inappropriate, harassing, or sexually suggestive, the recording can be used to prove or disprove the claim.

A disadvantage to recording is the intimidation that the examinee might feel. This can be minimized if the recording equipment is small, quiet, and unobtrusive. The less noticeable, the better. Also better is a longer recording tape that will need changing less often. Adequate equipment can commonly resolve any distraction that recording might otherwise cause.

Although audiotaping is easier and the equipment is simpler and less expensive, videotaping captures a great deal more information. Both video- and audiotape will record what is said, including voice inflections; videotape will also record what is done, including gestures, facial expressions, posture, movements, attentiveness, clothing, and grooming.

If videotaping is used, then a clock and a daily calendar can be placed on the wall or table so that the videotape will show the time and date and that no sections were removed from the videotape. Some sophisticated videorecorders have a clock and calendar built into the recording, and the time and date appears on the screen when it is viewed.

A 6- to 8-hour nonstop videorecorder can be rigged by putting an endless tape in a camcorder and wiring the camcorder into a videocassette recorder (VCR), the type most people have in their living rooms. The VCR can be set on slow recording speed. A videotape in a camcorder can be made endless simply by cutting the tape.

A small palmcorder can be used in place of a large camcorder. Battery operated palmcorders that can record nonstop for five hours are now available. It can be used with a small tabletop tripod so that it is barely noticeable.

A more expensive but simpler video option is a security surveillance videorecording system.

A recording does not replace notes. Taking notes in some form is advisable. Notes can be taken in handwriting or on a laptop computer or word processor. A more tedious method is to make notes while listening to or watching the recording after the examination is completed.

The examiner's raw notes, audio- or videotape, and final report are all part of his medical records of the case. All are discoverable. All should be preserved, protected, and kept confidential, just like any other medical records.

The examiner should keep his original raw notes and original recording. He should send his original final report to the attorney who retained him. He should, of course, keep a copy of that report. When the raw notes and the recording are released, only copies should be released.

Consent is advised for audio- or videorecording of an examination. It is less disruptive to turn on the recording equipment before the examinee is brought into the room. However, it is then prudent to promptly advise the examinee that the recording is being made and obtain the consent.

PSYCHOLOGICAL TESTS

Psychological testing can be included as part of a forensic psychiatry evaluation. Some forensic psychiatrists always include them, some never include them, and others include them sometimes. Each forensic expert decides for himself, case by case, whether he will include psychological tests in his evaluation.

The advantages of including psychological tests include (1) data that are more easily measurable and reproducible, (2) conclusions that are standardized, and (3) if a psychologist administers the tests, then another forensic expert is involved and can testify, which makes the conclusions more credible.

The disadvantages of including psychological tests include (1) additional time and expense, (2) too much data might produce, or appear to produce, inconsistencies in the findings, and (3) if a psychologist administers the tests, the involvement of the additional forensic expert can be divisive instead of complementary.

Some forensic psychiatrists themselves administer psychological tests. These are commonly the more familiar ones, such as the MMPI, which can be computer scored, and the Halstead-Reitan, which is relatively easy to correctly administer.

If psychological testing is included in a forensic psychiatry evaluation, then the conclusions of the tests should be included in the written report. Whether the raw data of the psychological test is included in the report is up to the examiner. The raw data will have to be available for the opposing side to examine at the time of a deposition or in response to an appropriate request.

Psychological test results are especially helpful in adding validity to a personality disorder diagnosis. Neuropsychological tests are especially helpful in adding validity to a brain injury or brain deficit diagnosis.

COLLATERAL EXAMINATIONS

There are times when it is prudent to interview informants in addition to the examinee. Information from relatives, friends, coworkers, and other observers is often very helpful. However, it is also suspect, depending on the agenda of the informant. The information gathered from informants can be used to determine the reputation, behavior patterns, and the personality characteristics of the evaluee observed by others. The obvious example is the gathering of information from family and friends regarding the testamentary capacity of a deceased "examinee." The forensic psychiatrist can recommend to the retaining attorney whether any such people should be included in the evaluation process of a case.

The referring attorney has the duty to determine whether such collateral examinations will be strategically helpful to his side. The attorney may prefer to include or exclude some collateral examinations. Which collateral examinations to include is the referring attorney's decision.

Collateral examinations should be conducted with the same care as examinations of a plaintiff or defendant examinee. Collateral examinees should be treated with the same respect and privacy as plaintiff or defendant examinees. They should be properly warned about the absence of confidentiality and they should not be given any confidential information.

Team Evaluations

The forensic psychiatrist can decide to use an evaluation team rather than perform the examination alone. The team can include psychologists and social workers. Social workers usually perform the best psychosocial evaluations. The team can also include other evaluators appropriate to a particular case, for example, a neurologist, an education specialist, or a rehabilitation expert.

The team should produce a single report with a single conclusion. Any conflicts in the findings of the various team members should be addressed in the report.

The advantages and disadvantages of using a team approach are the same as those listed above regarding the use of psychologists to do psychological testing.

Six

WRITING REPORTS

PURPOSE OF REPORTS

The purpose of a report is to document the findings and conclusions of the forensic psychiatrist. Sometimes the report is the only opportunity for communication that the expert witness has in a case. The report speaks for the expert witness. It is relied upon as a representation of the expert's findings and conclusions. Sometimes cases are settled or dropped on the basis of such written reports. Therefore it is important to prepare the report carefully; it should be precise and free of errors.

FORMAT

The first page of the report should be on letterhead stationery. It should begin with the name and address of the retaining attorney (or other party) to whom the report is written. The beginning of the text should then describe the reason for the evaluation and state who requested the evaluation.

The beginning should also list the materials reviewed as part of the evaluation. The list of materials should be detailed enough to enable readers to determine if those materials are also in their files.

It should not be so detailed, however, that it describes the content or conclusions of the materials.

The report should state the time and place of any examination of the evaluee or other examinees. If anyone else was present during an examination, that should also be stated.

The narrative then commences. It is easier to read if it is divided into sections, using introductory sentences and section headings. A sample format is outlined below. The report should contain the first three parts of a SOAP note: It should clearly indicate if material is subjective, objective, or a conclusion/assessment (a treatment plan is generally not a part of a forensic psychiatric report; it is not for treatment purposes).

Introduction
Materials reviewed
Information from examinee
    Illness or injury in question
    Treatments for this illness or injury
    Medical history
    Psychiatric history
    History of legal aspects of this case
    Personal history
    Family history
Observations
    Mental status examination
    Physical presentation of examinee
    Mental presentation of examinee
Conclusions
    Psychodynamic formulation
    Answers to attorney's questions

There are times when it is appropriate to address a report, "To Whom It May Concern," such as when a report is requested by multiple parties or the report is to be used for multiple purposes (a lawsuit, a criminal charge, a licensure investigation, and an insurance claim). A cover letter should accompany the report each time it is sent.

Attaching a CV (curriculum vitae) to a report when it is mailed is helpful. It saves the referring attorney from having to separately request it. It also lends validity to the report.

CONTENT

Some authors include all available data in their written reports. However, it is generally considered appropriate to leave out data that is irrelevant, especially if it is prejudicial. Some judgment is required in determining what data are irrelevant. Relevancy varies with the purpose of the evaluation and the questions being asked by the party requesting the evaluation.

Conclusory reports are commonly ill-advised. Conclusory reports list only the evaluator's conclusion, leaving out the data on which the conclusions are based and the reasoning that leads to the conclusions. Both the data on which conclusions are based and the reasoning of the evaluator are considered essential in written forensic reports.

GRAMMAR

Obviously, correct grammar in a report bespeaks the carefulness, knowledge, and education of the author. If an expert witness is unsure of his use of grammar, tenses, spelling, sentence structure, etc., he would be wise to have an editor review his reports before they are distributed. Some attorneys do this.

The introduction and conclusions may be written in the first person, for example, "I was asked by Attorney Alan Apple to evaluate Mr. Michael Martin" or "It is my opinion that this examinee has generalized anxiety disorder." The remainder of the report should be written in the third person, except for direct quotes. An example is:

He reports that his sleep pattern is backward, "I sleep from 1 to 5 every afternoon. I can't sleep at night."

READABILITY

In addition to being grammatically correct, an expert witness's report should be readable. Topic headings make reports easier to read. No sentence should be longer than 25–30 words. No paragraph should be longer than 8–10 sentences. Each paragraph should address one topic, not several. Paragraphs of one sentence are more readable than paragraphs of 30 sentences.

Simple sentences are easier to read than complex sentences. Note the differences between these two paragraphs:

The examinee attributes many symptoms to his upset over his unfair employment termination and he sleeps only four hours per night, taking two hours to fall asleep and awakening two hours before his alarm clock rings, being unable to fall back to sleep after the four hours and then he is tired during the day due to this pattern of insomnia.

The examinee attributes many symptoms to his upset over his unfair employment termination. It takes him two hours to fall asleep. He awakens two hours before his alarm clock rings. He sleeps only four hours per night. He is unable to fall back to sleep after the four hours. He is tired during the day due to this pattern of insomnia.

HOW TO REFER TO THE EXAMINEE

Some forensic psychiatrists name the examinee repeatedly throughout the report, for example, "Mr. Martin reports that his sleep pattern is backward." Some list the name of the examinee at the beginning of the report and then refer to him as the examinee, the subject, the defendant, the deceased, the employee, or some similar appropriate term. A report is easier to understand if the same term is used throughout the entire report. There appears to be no consensus about the best way of referring to the examinee.

TIMING

Some forensic psychiatrists prefer to complete their reports as soon as the examination is completed. They schedule time to do this, scheduling nothing else for the hour or two after an examination. This enables the evaluator to complete his report and conclusions while the examination is still fresh in his mind.

Others prefer to wait a few days before writing their conclusions. This gives them time to think about the data and be satisfied with their conclusions before writing and distributing the report.

Of course, most retaining attorneys want an expert's report immediately. A report should not be released, however, until the expert witness is satisfied that he can testify under oath as to its contents, particularly its conclusions.

SPECIFICITY

The more specific an expert witness is in reporting his findings, the clearer the picture in the mind of the reader. The second description below is an example of specificity.

```
The examinee sleeps poorly.
```

```
The examinee typically gets in bed at 10 p.m. but
does not fall asleep until 1 a.m. He then sleeps
restlessly, awakening approximately every hour. He
then awakens about 5 a.m., unable to fall back to
sleep before his alarm clock rings at 6 a.m. He feels
tired during the day.
```

The more specific an expert witness can be in his descriptions and conclusions, the less room there is for misinterpretation, misunderstanding, and manipulation of the data.

There are times when a vague answer is used intentionally to allow room for misinterpretation on the part of the reader. For example, in a wrongful death case, the conclusion of the plaintiff's forensic psychiatrist might be, "Mr. Martin is devastated by the unexpected death of his wife and the violent manner in which it occurred." This conclusion leaves a great deal of room for the imagination of the reader to fill in the blanks with all kinds of horrible images. However, it also leaves open the possibility that Mr. Martin has no depression or significant personal injury from the wrongful death. A vague conclusion leaves a great deal of clarifying to be done during cross-examination.

REPEAT THE QUESTION IN THE ANSWER

Conclusions are much easier to understand if they are divided into their individual questions. The clearest way to document conclusions is to state the question, then answer the question. Numbering the questions adds even greater clarity.

The simpler the question, the better. Simple questions can be answered with simple answers. Simple answers are difficult to misinterpret, misunderstand, and manipulate. Complex questions and answers, on the other hand, are hard to understand and easy to manipulate.

ANSWER EVERY QUESTION ASKED

Obviously, the expert witness should address in his written report every question asked by the referring attorney.

Sometimes questions are asked by the referring attorney in a vague, complicated, or compound fashion. Answers are much clearer if the expert witness breaks down the question into its many parts. Then the expert witness can address each single question individually. For example, the following complex question can be broken down into a list of simple questions when the expert witness writes his conclusions:

```
Is Mr. Martin totally and permanently disabled due
to his work-related depressive illness?

1. What is the psychiatric diagnosis of the exami-
   nee?
2. Was this psychiatric condition caused by his
   employment at the ABC Company?
3. Is the examinee disabled by this psychiatric con-
   dition?
4. Is this disability total?
5. Is this disability permanent?
```

Of course, each answer should be explained so that it can stand on its own, without requiring further verbal explanation. (The report as a whole should also be able to stand by itself, without requiring further explanation.)

Another example of a question that requires breaking down into parts is a question about multiple counts of criminal charges. The following question should be broken down into its multiple parts when answered:

```
Was Mr. Martin able to appreciate the nature and
quality, or the wrongfulness, of his acts, and was
he able to conform his conduct to the requirements
of the law when he committed the three incidents of
assault and battery?

1. The examinee is criminally responsible for the
   first count of assault and battery. It occurred
   while he was conscious, aware of the situation at
   hand, and free of the influence of any mind-
   altering substances. He was able, at that time,
   to control his behavior and conform his conduct
```

to the requirements of the law. He admits that he
was aware, at that time, that his behavior was
unlawful. He admits that he was aware, at the
time he threw the log at Mr. Smith, that his
behavior would likely cause substantial injury
to Mr. Smith.

2. The examinee is not criminally responsible for
the second count of assault and battery. He did
not know that Mr. Timmer had put rocks in the
water balloons. He thought that he was throwing
water balloons that were just water balloons,
similar to the water balloons that the child was
throwing at him. He did not know that his throwing the water balloon would injure the child. He
did not appreciate the nature and quality, or
wrongfulness, of his behavior because he did not
know of the rocks in the water balloons.

   The examinee was able to conform his conduct
to the requirements of the law. He thought that
he was doing so. He thought that the balloons
were safe, his behaviors were safe, and that he
would not harm the child by throwing the water
balloons at the child.

   The question of criminal intent appears to be
more relevant than the question of criminal
responsibility regarding this second count of
assault and battery. The examinee did not intend
to harm the child, just as the child did not
intend to harm the examinee, as they were play-
fully throwing water balloons at each other.

3. The examinee is not criminally responsible for
the third count of assault and battery. At the
time of this event, the examinee was under the
influence of the LSD that had been put into his
lemonade by Mr. Underwood. The examinee did not
know about the LSD. The examinee saw that Mr.

Underwood was about to shoot him with handguns, and so protected himself by trying to knock the guns out of Mr. Underwood's hands with the baseball bat. Of course, the handguns were a hallucination caused by the involuntary consumption of LSD.

The examinee was not aware that his perceptions were inaccurate. He thought that his behavior was self-defense. He did appreciate that his behavior would likely injure Mr. Underwood, but he knew that injuring another person in self-defense is not unlawful. Thus, he did not appreciate, due to the hallucination caused by the LSD, that the nature and quality of his conduct were unlawful, and that it was based upon his incorrect perception. He believed he was acting in self-defense, and therefore thought he was conforming his conduct to the requirements of the law.

All three answers address both legs of the criminal responsibility statute. All six questions are addressed separately.

Answer 2 addresses a very relevant question that was not overtly asked. The question becomes obvious, however, in the answer to the question that was asked. When it becomes obvious that the question of criminal responsibility is not applicable to the second count of assault and battery, the question about assault and battery is addressed anyway, because it was asked. But then the successive relevant question about criminal intent is addressed, in order to give a complete answer to the implied question. The implied question is: If the question of criminal responsibility does not apply to the second count of assault and battery, then did the examinee intend the harm he perpetrated in the assault and battery?

It is important to address each leg of the statute separately for each count of assault and battery. This is because a factfinder might agree with some of the expert witness's conclusions, and disagree with others. The factfinder might have doubts about some conclusions, but not others. If the expert witness addresses all six questions in one answer, then a factfinder who disagrees with one part of the conclusion is likely to discard the entire conclusion. If the expert witness addresses each part of each question individually, then the factfinder can discard only those conclusions with which he disagrees, and he can embrace those answers with which he agrees.

It is permissible to address questions in groups if the same answer applies to all the questions. Here is an example:

> Was the examinee criminally responsible for the 20 instances of assault and battery he committed on January 1, 1996? Criminal responsibility requires that a person appreciate the nature and quality, or wrongfulness, of his acts, and that the person is able to conform his conduct to the requirements of the law.
>
> The examinee is not criminally responsible for all 20 counts of assault and battery. At the time of all 20 of the events in question, the examinee was under the influence of the LSD that had been put into his lemonade by Mr. Underwood. The examinee did not know about the LSD. The examinee thought that all 20 people he attacked were coming at him with hunting knives. Of course, they were not, but he perceived this due to his involuntarily consumed LSD.
>
> The examinee was not aware that his perceptions were inaccurate. He thought that his behavior was self-defense. He did appreciate that his behavior would likely injure all 20 of the assailants, but he was aware that injuring others in self-defense is not unlawful. Thus, he did not appreciate, due to the hallucination caused by the LSD, that the nature and quality of his behavior were unlawful. He did not appreciate that his behavior was based upon his incorrect perception.

The examinee thought he was acting in self-
defense. He thought he was conforming his conduct
to the requirements of the law.

It is permissible to distribute a report without conclusions. The conclusions section might say: "I am unable to draw my conclusions regarding this case at this time. More information is needed before I can do so." This is sometimes done when the expert wishes to discuss his conclusions with the referring attorney before writing and distributing them.

STORAGE OF RECORDS

Forensic psychiatry reports are considered attorney work product (see pages 70–71) or the property of the party requesting the evaluation.

The records of a forensic psychiatry case are confidential, like medical records. They should be protected from the view of others such as janitors, trash collectors, and other professional and clerical people who have no involvement in the case.

Records should be stored with the same care and security as medical records are stored.

HOW LONG TO KEEP RECORDS

There is no established period of time a physician must keep office medical records. A forensic psychiatrist must keep his forensic records a *reasonable* amount of time. There is no standard as to how long that is. It is permissible to ask a referring attorney at the end of a case if the records may be destroyed. Even if the records are destroyed, it is wise to keep formal reports for two years after a case is closed. Two years is the statute of limitations for medical malpractice lawsuits (in Michigan; it may be different in other states).

If there is no action on a forensic file for two years, it is reasonable to ask the attorney if the records should be kept longer or destroyed.

DISTRIBUTING REPORTS

An expert witness may distribute his report by U.S. mail, express mail, courier, or by directly handing it to the referring attorney. Reports may also be rendered via e-mail or fax, or by phone or direct conversation; in these cases, a hard copy of the written report, signed by the expert witness, is also required.

As with any medical report, confidentiality must be protected.

The information in the report is "owned" by the referring attorney, the party requesting the forensic evaluation. The report is not to be released to the examinee, or any other party, without the consent of the referring attorney.

Forensic psychiatry evaluations do not commonly include treatment recommendations; it is, however, acceptable to include them. If treatment recommendations are urgent, then the referring attorney's consent for release of that information should be obtained, and the treatment recommendations should then be released to the appropriate provider of treatment. The expert witness should not become the provider of treatment.

If it is appropriate for the forensic psychiatrist to send a copy of his report to the examinee's attending physician, that may be done, but only with the consent of the referring attorney and the examinee.

As with any medical report, the forensic psychiatrist should keep a copy for his own file.

ATTORNEY WORK PRODUCT

The expert witness's report, and all the information and opinions the expert has about a case, are considered attorney work product.

Attorney work product is the information that an attorney has about a case. Such information is privileged and not discoverable.

The expert witness is not to release any information or opinions about a case without the consent of the retaining attorney or a court order. Commonly, such information is released only to the retaining attorney or only in a deposition or trial attended by the retaining attorney. The retaining attorney, of course, is allowed to release the expert witness's information and opinions as he wishes, pursuant to his purposes and within his legal limitations.

TEMPLATE FOR REPORTS

In the career of a forensic psychiatrist, the writing of reports is probably the most influential activity performed. Most cases are settled by the attorneys after the written reports of the experts are rendered. Only a small percentage of cases progress to trial after the experts render their reports.

Because the expert witness's reports are so influential in the disposition of cases, several examples of written reports are offered in appendix D.

The following is an example of a template that can be used on a computer. With such a template, report writing becomes an easy exercise of filling in the blanks. The computer can be programmed to go to the next blank upon the completion of the previous blank. This can be easily done in a word processing program by using the merge function. This is the template used for the criminal defense report on George Gunner in appendix D. [KEYBOARD] designates the place to which the computer takes the typist for the next blank to be filled in.

Some of the [KEYBOARD] locations are places where changes are to be made only if the examinee's case differs from that already typed into the template. If no changes are needed, then the examiner can simply go on the next [KEYBOARD] location. If changes are needed, then the changes are entered, including deleting the nonapplicable templated words. Then the examiner moves to the next [KEYBOARD] location.

[DATE CODE]
[KEYBOARD]
Re: [KEYBOARD]

CONFIDENTIAL PSYCHIATRIC REPORT

At your request, I performed a psychiatric evaluation of the above named subject, [KEYBOARD], in my office on [KEYBOARD]. This examination is videotaped.

For your reference, a copy of my current curriculum vitae is attached.

Prior to my examination of the subject, I reviewed the several documents that you sent. They are:

1. [KEYBOARD]
2. [KEYBOARD]

I used the content of these documents to prepare for myself a list of questions to ask the subject. I did not rely upon the content of these documents in reaching my conclusions regarding this case.

At the beginning of my examination, I explained to the subject the nature of the examination and the absence of the usual medical confidentiality. The subject agreed to proceed with the examination with those understandings.

The following are my findings and conclusions regarding my evaluation of this subject.

HISTORY OF INJURY

The following is the history of the injury in question, as told to me by the subject.

The subject is age [KEYBOARD].

EFFECTS

The following is the history of the effects of the injuries in question, as told to me by the subject. [KEYBOARD]

TREATMENTS

The following is the history of the treatments received for the injuries in question, as told to me by the subject.

The doctor presently treating the subject is [KEYBOARD].

MEDICAL HISTORY

The following is the medical history of this subject, in addition to the above, as told to me by the subject.

The subject's general doctor is [KEYBOARD].

In a typical day, the subject smokes [KEYBOARD] packs of cigarettes. In a typical week, the subject's alcohol consumption is [KEYBOARD]. The last time the subject used street drugs was [KEYBOARD].

The medications the subject presently takes are [KEYBOARD].

PSYCHIATRIC ASPECTS OF THIS CASE

The following is the history of the psychiatric aspects of this case, as told to me by the subject.

The psychiatrist presently treating the subject is [KEYBOARD].

The subject has never been seen by any psychiatrist, psychologist, social worker, or counselor of any sort, other than the above.

With regard to sleep, the subject [KEYBOARD].

With regard to appetite, the subject [KEYBOARD].

With regard to memory functioning and concentration ability, the subject [KEYBOARD].

With regard to depressed mood, the subject [KEYBOARD].

At this point, the subject's usual daily activities consist of [KEYBOARD].

The subject's hobbies and special interests are [KEYBOARD].

With regard to loss of interest in hobbies and usual activities, the subject [KEYBOARD].

The subject denies any history of suicidal thoughts or suicide attempts. [KEYBOARD] If the subject were to attempt suicide today, the method he would use would be, "[KEYBOARD]."

The subject denies any history of symptoms of hallucinations or delusions. [KEYBOARD]

With regard to loss of energy, the subject [KEYBOARD].

With regard to feelings of worthlessness, the subject [KEYBOARD].

With regard to slowed movements, the subject [KEYBOARD].

The subject denies the symptoms of mania. [KEYBOARD]

In general, the subject would describe himself, presently, as a person who is, "[KEYBOARD]."

In general, the subject would describe himself as a person who was, about [KEYBOARD] years ago, "[KEYBOARD]."

LEGAL ASPECTS OF THIS CASE

The following are the legal aspects of this case, as told to me by the subject.

The attorney representing the subject is [KEYBOARD].

The subject presently supports himself with [KEYBOARD].

The subject has never been sued by any party. He has never sued any party. He has never been in jail. [KEYBOARD]

The subject got to my office for this psychiatric appointment by driving himself, alone, in his own car. He is able to drive with no problem. [KEYBOARD]

PERSONAL AND FAMILY HISTORY

The following is the personal and family history of this subject, as told to me by the subject.

The subject was born on [KEYBOARD].

The subject's mother is [KEYBOARD].

The subject's father is [KEYBOARD].

The subject's siblings are [KEYBOARD].

The subject is married [KEYBOARD].

The children the subject has are [KEYBOARD].

With regard to whether religion plays an important part in this subject's life, [KEYBOARD].

MENTAL STATUS EXAMINATION

The following are the answers given by the subject to my asking him the questions in a standard mental status examination.

The date is, "[KEYBOARD]." I am, "[KEYBOARD]." This room is, "[KEYBOARD]." The presidents in reverse order are, "[KEYBOARD]." Serially subtracting $7 from $100, "[KEYBOARD]."

If the subject were walking down the street and found a letter lying next to a mailbox, he would, "[KEYBOARD]." If the subject were in a theater and saw the curtains on fire, he would, "[KEYBOARD]." If someone said to the subject that the grass is always greener on the other side of the fence, that person would be trying to say, "[KEYBOARD]." If someone said, don't cry over spilled milk, that would mean, "[KEYBOARD]."

OBJECTIVE OBSERVATIONS

The following are my objective observations regarding this subject.

The subject was present on schedule [KEYBOARD] for his psychiatric examination. He was appropriately [KEYBOARD] dressed in [KEYBOARD]. The general appearance of this subject is that of a [KEYBOARD].

The subject is alert, oriented, appropriate, calm, cooperative, likeable, and friendly. [KEYBOARD] His affect (observed mood) is not depressed, angry, or anxious. [KEYBOARD] He is easily able to express himself verbally. [KEYBOARD] He is appropriately able to laugh and smile. [KEYBOARD]

The subject exhibits no apparent movement disorders, gait disturbances, or general discomforts. [KEYBOARD]

My examination of the subject began at [KEYBOARD] and ended at [KEYBOARD] on [KEYBOARD], and on [KEYBOARD] it began at [KEYBOARD] and ended at [KEYBOARD].

DISCUSSION

The following is my explanation of the psychodynamic status of this subject.
[KEYBOARD]

CONCLUSIONS

The following are my answers to your questions, as an independent forensic psychiatric examiner, regarding this subject, based upon the above history and findings.

1.   [KEYBOARD]
2.   [KEYBOARD]

If I can clarify any of my findings or conclusions for you, or address any further questions, I will be happy to hear from you.

I do give you my consent to release copies of this report to any party you judge to be appropriate.

Thank you for having referred this very interesting subject to me for psychiatric evaluation.

Sincerely yours,

Steven H. Berger, M.D.
enc.

Seven

SUBPOENAS

A subpoena is an order issued by a judge or an attorney for a person or medical records to appear at a designated time and place. There is commonly no penalty for failing to respond to a subpoena issued by an attorney. There is, however, usually a penalty for failing to respond to a subpoena issued by a judge. Failing to fulfill a judge's subpoena is considered to be contempt of court. A judge can order a fine or incarceration for contempt of court.

A subpoena from a judge often has the judge's stamp instead of his signature. Such a subpoena carries the same weight as if the judge had signed it.

TYPES

There are basically two types of subpoenas, to produce records (duces tecum) or to appear in person. The subpoena to produce records sent to a forensic psychiatrist usually requires him to send copies of his office records to the person issuing the subpoena. Often, the retaining attorney will either quash (invalidate) such a subpoena, answer the subpoena himself, or instruct the expert witness to go ahead and comply with the subpoena.

A subpoena to appear requires the recipient to be present at the prescribed time and place. Such subpoenas commonly are for testimony at a deposition or trial, and require a person to bring case records with him.

RESPONSES

Unless the subpoena is signed by a judge, the forensic psychiatrist may be breaching confidentiality if he releases records or information without proper consent. Proper consent would come from (1) the person about whom the medical records are written, (2) the retaining attorney, or (3) the attorney representing the person about whom the medical records are written (the subject of the medical records).

Even with appropriate consent, it is improper for one physician to release the records of any other physician, hospital, or provider. A physician may properly release only his own records.

When releasing records in response to a subpoena or any other request, only copies should be released. A physician should always retain his original records, except as noted in chapter 6; the original draft of the expert's report should be given to the retaining attorney and a copy kept in the psychiatrist's office chart.

A subpoena to appear requires a person to be present at the designated time and place. Such a subpoena, however, does not require a person to testify. He can refuse to testify: He might prefer not to testify or might be breaching confidentiality by testifying. If a person refuses to testify and the judge then orders him to do so, he will be in contempt of court if he does not.

If a subpoena requires both attendance and records, then the person should bring his records with him. It is wise to also bring a photocopy of the records that are likely to be kept by the court. When the forensic psychiatrist is then asked to turn his records over to the court, he can ask to be allowed to turn over photocopies so he can keep his originals. That is usually allowed.

Similar to appearing and then refusing to testify, a physician can bring his case records but refuse to turn them over to the court. The same principles prevail. If the judge orders the physician to surrender his records, then the physician is in contempt of court if he fails to do so.

There are times when a forensic psychiatrist would prefer not to turn over records or testify. In such cases, it is preferable to be court ordered to turn records over to the court or to testify. Examples of such situations are (1) the forensic psychiatrist has information that is damaging to his side of the case, (2) the physician does not have proper consent to release the information, or (3) the expert witness no longer wants to be involved in the case for whatever reason.

Eight

DEPOSITIONS

ATTENDEES

A deposition is testimony rendered in an office setting rather than a courtroom. At any deposition, there is commonly an attorney representing each party to the litigation, a court reporter, and the deponent. The deponent is the person testifying, the person being deposed. In civil cases, the plaintiff or the defendant might also be present at a deposition.

There are times when some of the parties to a litigation are not represented at a deposition. When the expert witness's retaining attorney is absent, the expert should not proceed with the deposition. Proceeding with a deposition in the absence of other attorneys is permissible.

PURPOSE OF A DEPOSITION

Depositions of expert witnesses serve two purposes: discovery (called a discovery deposition) and preservation of testimony (called a trial deposition). A discovery deposition is commonly requested by the opposing side in a litigation. The purpose of a discovery deposition is for the other side to (1) learn what a witness is going to testify at the trial, and (2) learn about the witness.

One reason the opposing side seeks to know an opposing witness's testimony is to evaluate the strength of the other side's case.

After the strength or weakness of the other side's case is known, the case might be settled based on the anticipated outcome of a trial.

Another reason to learn the other side's testimony is to prepare to respond to it at the trial. The response might be to challenge the expert, present opposing data, present opposing testimony by other witnesses, or not to respond to it at all. The reason to avoid responding to damaging testimony is to avoid drawing the jury's attention to it, and thereby avoid making it even more damaging to one's own side.

The reason the opposing side seeks to learn about the witness is to be prepared to discredit the witness at the trial. In discovery depositions, it is common for the opposing attorney to ask the expert witness his credentials, training, job history, publications, professional activities, professional positions held, honors, and similar professional information commonly included in a curriculum vitae. The opposing attorney also commonly asks about any disciplinary actions, license limitations or losses, staff privilege limitations or losses, malpractice claims and outcomes, felony charges, ethics investigations, and any other shameful information or information damaging to one's credibility and reputation.

In order to learn any other ways to make the expert witness look less credible on the witness stand, the opposing attorney will commonly ask if the expert is board certified, and how many tries it took the expert to pass the board tests. Other similar questions might assess the number of cases the expert has evaluated for the retaining attorney, how often the expert's testimony has favored the plaintiff or defense, whether the expert has any prejudices, how much the expert is getting paid, etc.

It is generally best to answer such questions honestly and directly. If the expert witness has anything to hide, it should have been discussed with the referring attorney when the expert agreed to work on the case. How to handle skeletons in the expert witness's closet, or other damaging information, is a matter of strategy to be determined by the retaining attorney.

Particular topics of inquiry might occur, depending on the case at hand. For example, in a child custody case, the expert witness might be asked if he is married or divorced, if he has children, if he has custody of his children, if he feels that children should always be in the custody of their mothers, etc. The expert's position on such questions can bolster or injure his credibility. Again, the retaining attorney makes the strategic decisions regarding how inquiries about such matters should be handled.

The other purpose of a deposition is to preserve testimony. A deposition for this purpose is called a trial deposition. Such depositions are commonly arranged by the retaining attorney. In these, the expert witness testifies as if at the trial. If the expert is unable to attend the trial for any reason, then his trial deposition can be read at the trial.

When a trial deposition transcript is read at a trial, the retaining attorney will read his questions from the deposition transcript, and someone, commonly an employee from the attorney's office, will sit in the witness stand and read the expert's answers from the deposition transcript. The intent is to present to the jury the expert witness's testimony, as if the expert were there in the courtroom testifying live.

Often, trial depositions are videotaped. Videotaped depositions are commonly better received by juries. Instead of the expert witness being in the witness stand listening to questions and verbalizing answers live, he is doing so on television. It is easy for jurors to comprehend that the person on television is the person rendering the opinions. It is somewhat dissonant for a juror to watch a person in the witness stand reading someone else's answers to questions asked by the attorney.

In a videotaped deposition, the expert should look into the camera when answering questions: The jury will be better able to pay attention to the expert when they watch the deposition on television from the jury box. Obviously, in a videotaped deposition, the expert should take the procedure very seriously, as if he is indeed on the witness stand, live at a trial.

Time and Place

The time and place of a deposition are usually arranged by mutual agreement between all the attorneys and the expert witness. Often, the retaining attorney will arrange with the expert witness, or the expert's secretary, for the time and place to hold the deposition. The retaining attorney will then notify the other attorneys. The attorney who is requesting the deposition arranges for the court reporter.

The deposition is most often held in the expert witness's office. It can also be held in an attorney's office, a hotel conference room, a hotel sleeping room, a hospital conference room, or any other place the attorney might arrange.

Sometimes a deposition is scheduled by the opposing attorney without the agreement of the expert witness. When this occurs, the expert will commonly be subpoenaed by the opposing attorney to attend the deposition. Whether the expert attends a deposition under these circumstances is a matter of strategy to be determined by the retaining attorney.

It is permissible for the expert witness to limit the length of a deposition. For example, if the deposition is scheduled for up to three hours, and it is incomplete at that point, the expert can stop the proceedings and invite the attorneys to continue at some future time. The future time is then arranged in the same way the initial deposition time was arranged.

Often, expert witnesses prefer to schedule depositions for the end of the day. That way, it can continue until it is completed, no matter how long it takes.

THE COURT REPORTER

The court reporter transcribes the deposition word for word. The attorney calling for the deposition arranges for the court reporter and pays the reporter's fees.

The court reporter prepares a deposition transcript. The deponent, the expert witness, has the right to read and sign the transcript. Some experts routinely waive that right.

If the expert does read and sign the deposition transcript, he may not change the content of it. If he has any corrections to make, he may submit them to the retaining attorney as addenda to the transcript.

Sometimes a court recorder is used instead of a court reporter. A court recorder uses audiorecording or videorecording equipment instead of a transcription machine.

PREPARATION

The expert witness should prepare for a deposition as studiously as he prepares for a trial. Testimony given in a deposition is no less significant than that given at trial. Anything said in a deposition can be presented in a trial and used either to support or to impeach a witness.

Preparation includes reviewing all relevant notes and discussing the case with the attorney. The discussion can be by phone or in person, and should include the questions that will be asked of the witness by both sides and the answers that the witness will give. The discussion should be sufficiently complete such that no surprise questions or answers occur in the deposition.

The expert witness should bring to the deposition his entire file on the case and any reference materials he plans to use, such as the *DSM-IV*, textbooks, or relevant articles. Bringing a copy of one's curriculum vitae and a list of past testimonies (see below) is also helpful.

BREAKS

It is permissible for the deponent to ask to take a break in a deposition at any time after he has answered a question. Once a question has been asked, it must be answered before a break can be taken.

Sometimes a line of questioning by an attorney is so rapid that the witness does not have a chance to say that he wants to take a break. In response to the next question, the witness can say, "After I answer this question, I want to take a break." Then he can answer the question, and then a break can be taken.

Reasons to take breaks are to answer a pager, place or receive a phone call, confer with the retaining attorney regarding a line of questioning, use the bathroom, have lunch, have a cigarette, or just have time to take a break. When questioning is rapid and the questions are difficult, a break might be taken by the witness just to compose himself.

If an expert does not know the answer to a question, then the best answer generally is, "I don't know." If an answer is speculative, or a guess, then the expert should state so as part of his answer.

PAYMENT

It is prudent for an expert witness to require payment in advance for deposition time for two reasons. One reason is to assure payment. The more important reason, however, is to allow the expert witness to be honest. The retaining attorney expects testimony supportive of his side. Information might be presented in a deposition that changes the expert's opinion to one that is supportive of the other side. If this happens, and the expert has not been paid in advance, then the retaining attorney may refuse to pay the expert. If the expert is paid in advance for his time, then he can concern himself with giving honest testimony. If he is not paid in advance, his greatest concern might be whether the retaining attorney is going to like his testimony. The ethical forensic psychiatrist must be honest and strive for objectivity.

The amount of prepayment can be estimated, based on the anticipated length of the deposition. Overpayment should, of course, be refunded to the payer.

There are many exceptions to this recommendation for advance payment. The most common one is when the expert's bill is being paid by a defense insurance company. Insurance companies generally pay the bills of their expert witnesses without hassle. Another exception is an attorney with whom the expert has a longstanding, trusting relationship. Another exception is when the court is paying the expert's fee. Courts may withhold payment for other reasons, but rarely based on the content of the expert's testimony.

Sometimes the fee for a discovery deposition is paid by the opposing attorney, the one who requests the deposition. In such cases, it is permissible for the expert to refuse a deposition until after he is paid for his time.

Sometimes the opposing attorney will request some homework from the expert witness. The attorney might ask the expert to find a particular piece of medical literature, produce a list of cases in which he testified a particular way, deliver a photocopy of his file, or some similar task. The expert should assure that the opposing attorney will pay for the expert's time and expense of doing the homework. This can be accomplished by getting the attorney's assertion on the record that he will pay, getting payment in advance, or getting a letter from the attorney assuring payment. The best way to ensure payment is to get it in advance.

Advance payment for homework can be handled in this way: During the deposition, on the record, the opposing attorney will ask the expert witness for some homework. The expert can then say that he will do the homework, that he will require $XXX for the X number of hours it will take to do the work, and that payment must be received before the homework will be done.

A common question asked by opposing attorneys is, "Doctor, are you getting paid for your testimony here today?" The correct answer is, "No. I am getting paid for my time." Time is the only thing for which a forensic psychiatrist should be paid.

CONTENT AND SEQUENCE

A deposition starts with introductions. The expert will be asked to state his name, professional address, educational background, and other information commonly contained in a psychiatrist's curriculum vitae. Voir dire is the process of learning the qualifications of the expert witness.

Next, the expert is asked about the process of his evaluation of the case at hand, whether he examined the defendant or claimant, when, where, how long, etc. The expert is then asked his findings and opinions regarding the case.

The first attorney to ask questions is the attorney who requested the deposition. Then the attorney for each other party in the litigation has a turn to ask questions of the expert witness. This continues, in order, until there are no further questions.

Any attorney can raise an objection at any time. In a deposition, the objection is stated on the record. Then, unless the question is withdrawn, the witness answers the question, despite the objection. If the deposition is later read at the trial, any questions to which objections are sustained will not be read to the jury.

When answering questions, a witness should hesitate before answering. This gives the attorneys time to object before an answer is given. If an objection is raised, the witness should remain silent until directed to go ahead and answer the question.

There are rare times when the retaining attorney will direct an expert witness not to answer a question. This may occur because the question is illegal, argumentative, prejudicial, irrelevant, etc. The expert should follow the instructions of his retaining attorney.

It is prudent for an expert witness to answer only the question asked. Giving extra information can open the door to other areas of inquiry. Often, this turns out to be troublesome much more than it is helpful. When asked, "Do you know the date?" the correct answer is, "Yes." Giving the date is the wrong answer. The more common error is to offer one's opinion when asked, "Do you have an opinion regarding . . . ?" The correct answer is, "Yes." The wrong answer is to go ahead and give one's opinion.

The opposing attorney often asks the expert to list the opinions he intends to give at the trial. If the expert can give such a list, the deposition will run more smoothly and the essential points of the witness's testimony can be more directly addressed. Here is an example:

> Dr. Expert, what opinions do you intend to give at the malpractice trial regarding Dr. Blunder?
> Dr. Blunder's care of his patient, Mrs. Injured, fell below the standard of care in these ways:

1. He failed to return her phone call on January 10, 1996, in a reasonable amount of time.
2. He prescribed medication that is not commonly prescribed for her diagnosis.
3. He failed to treat her with medication that fulfills the standard of care for her diagnosis.

After the expert renders such a list, the opposing attorney will commonly ask if there are any other opinions the expert will give in the case. If the expert answers no, then the opposing attorney will object to any further opinions offered by the expert later. For this reason, it is appropriate for the expert to respond that, at this time, he knows of no other opinions he intends to offer in the case.

LISTS OF CASES

In federal cases, the opposing attorney is allowed to require an expert witness to list the federal cases in which he has testified in the last three years (see chapter 2 for further discussion). The expert can be asked for the name of the case, the case number, the retaining attorney, whether the retaining attorney represented the plaintiff or the defense, and the nature of the case.

It is wise for a forensic psychiatrist to keep a list containing this information. It is also wise to bring a copy of this list to depositions, along with one's curriculum vitae. Some forensic psychiatrists keep such a list for all cases, not just federal cases.

An expert witness is often asked in a deposition the number of cases of a particular sort in which he has served as an expert witness, and the side for which he testified. The purpose of this question is to determine whether the expert is prejudiced, for example, always testifying against a finding of not guilty by reason of insanity or always testifying in favor of the physician in malpractice cases. Some forensic psychiatrists keep such a list for reference purposes. Sometimes the list records only cases in which depositions occurred; other times, all cases, even when no deposition occurred, are included.

Sometimes an opposing attorney will ask in a deposition for a list of other attorneys or law firms that have retained the expert, and the types of cases involved. The above lists are helpful in answering such questions.

Nine

TRIALS

ROLE OF THE EXPERT WITNESS

Any trial can be viewed as simply a factual dispute. The role of the jury is to resolve the dispute, one way or another, and determine the facts of the case. The jury is the factfinder. No one else is the factfinder. In the absence of a jury, of course, the judge is the factfinder.

An expert witness is a person who has knowledge, training, or experience not held by the common juror. The role of the expert witness is to teach the jury that specialized knowledge so that the jury can determine the facts of the case. He is allowed to give opinion testimony based upon his specialized body of knowledge. His opinions are simply additional pieces of information to be considered by the jury.

The retaining attorney's role is to present the expert witness's opinions to the jury in the way most favorable to his side of the case. He does this by asking the expert questions during the trial. It is also the retaining attorney's role to do this with the greatest amount of credibility for the expert's opinions.

The opposing attorney's role is to get the expert witness to turn his testimony around so that it no longer supports the retaining attorney's side. It is also his role to reduce the credibility of the expert, in the eyes of the jury, as much as he can.

Thus, the role of the psychiatric expert witness in the courtroom is to teach the jury his opinions in a case and the knowledge upon which those opinions are based. He must do this within the rules and limitations of the court—which are often very frustrating for the inexperienced forensic psychiatrist.

SCHEDULING

Some courts are more accommodating than others. Sometimes an expert witness can be scheduled, for example, for 9:00 a.m. Tuesday morning. Often, courts will interrupt other witnesses in order to allow the physician expert witness to take the stand and testify, in accordance with the schedule prearranged by the attorneys.

Prearranged schedules are sometimes very closely followed, and sometimes they are not. It is prudent to plan extra time for court appearances. For example, if testimony is expected to take one or two hours, then planning to be at court for half a day is wise.

Other times, the courts or attorneys will not agree to a schedule. Then the expert witness must appear when the retaining attorney asks him to. This is disruptive to any person's schedule, which is the reason why some forensic psychiatrists do no clinical work— they find it impossible to schedule patients for treatment sessions when they can be called to appear in court at any time.

If a forensic psychiatrist knows that he is likely to be called to testify on June 15, then he can plan to schedule no patients on that day. If he then learns on June 12 that he will be in court on June 16 instead of June 15, he can then try to switch his June 16 patients to June 15. The helpful thing here is to leave enough time in one's schedule, and enough flexibility if possible, to accommodate the fluctuations of the court's schedule.

For out-of-town court appearances, it is wise to take along an extra day's clothes and toiletries, in case testimony takes more than one day.

Obviously, it is important to be prompt for court appearances. It is better to be 30 minutes early than 5 minutes late.

CLOTHING AND BEHAVIOR

The forensic psychiatrist is first a physician; second, a psychiatrist; third, a forensic psychiatrist; and fourth, an expert witness. As such, it is incumbent upon the forensic psychiatrist to dress and behave like a physician in the courtroom.

Although the physician may be the chief decision maker in his hospital or office, he is at the mercy of the judge in a courtroom. The expert witness should be respectful of the courtroom decorum and obedient to the judge.

Expert witnesses should remain silent while others are testifying. If any talking does occur, it should be in whispers. It is prudent to switch beepers to vibrating mode, and watches to nonchiming mode. Cellular phones should not ring. Of course, cellular phone calls should occur only outside, in the hallway, while the court is in session.

Male forensic psychiatrists should wear a suit and tie in court. Female forensic psychiatrists should dress in similar professional attire. Flashy, jangly, casual, or sexually provocative attire is out of place in the courtroom. Physicians' white coats are also out of place.

It is appropriate to address the judge as "Your honor" or "Judge."

WHEN AND WHERE TO WAIT

Expert witnesses spend a lot of time waiting in courthouses. In many cases, it is appropriate to sit in the audience section of the courtroom until called to the witness stand. In some cases, however, an attorney may object to an expert witness listening to the testimony of other witnesses. He may ask that the expert witness be sequestered, which means to wait out of hearing range while other witnesses are testifying. The most frequent instance is an attorney objecting to the other side's expert witness watching while his expert witness testifies. The retaining attorney may then ask his expert witness to wait in the hallway or other waiting area outside the courtroom. The expert witness should comply with such a request.

PREPARATION

The preparation and payment arrangements for a trial are the same as for depositions.

An expert witness should always read his deposition transcripts in preparation for the trial, sometimes more than once. This is important as a way of avoiding contradictions between deposition and court testimonies.

The expert witness need not bring his curriculum vitae and list of previous testimonies to the courtroom. If either attorney wants to have either one admitted into evidence, that attorney will bring it, having obtained it from a prior deposition or requested it prior to the trial.

It is permissible, and sometimes preferable, for a forensic psychiatrist witness to use a blackboard or other display in presenting his information to the jury. An example of a display is the listing of the diagnostic criteria for posttraumatic stress disorder; the expert can then check off the criteria fulfilled by the defendant. Using a display in this way makes testimony less confusing for the jury. Displays require some preparation. They should be prepared in advance, even professionally prepared by a display artist if appropriate. Of course, any displays should be arranged with the retaining attorney, who may also arrange for the preparation of the displays.

When testifying with the use of displays, it is permissible to stand up from the witness box and walk to the display, using the display as a lecture aide. This, of course, should be choreographed with the retaining attorney prior to the trial.

The expert witness may take whatever records he wishes to the witness stand. However, anything he takes to the witness stand may be kept by the court as an exhibit. It is wise to plan ahead, with the retaining attorney, what to take to the stand. It is also wise to take photocopies, not originals. Whatever the court keeps as exhibits might not be returned to the witness.

Breaks

Whereas it is common for an expert witness to ask for a break in a deposition, doing so in a courtroom is less common. The judge usually provides breaks every two hours or so. If needed for any reason, an expert witness can ask that the court take a break. He must do so after he answers a question that has already been asked; he cannot ask for a break before answering the question. It is fair to say, "I will answer this question, but then I need to take a break."

Content and Sequence

Court testimony follows the same sequence, and contains the same elements, as trial deposition testimony.

First, the retaining attorney calls the forensic psychiatrist to take the witness stand, "The defense calls Dr. John Smith." The forensic psychiatrist than walks to the witness stand with whatever materials he will need. Before he sits down, the judge asks the witness to raise his right hand and solemnly swear that he will tell the truth, the whole truth, and nothing but the truth. The witness replies, "I do" or "Yes" or "I so affirm." Then the witness is seated.

The retaining attorney will ask the witness his name and proceed with the same sequence of questions as in a trial deposition, starting with voir dire. Voir dire is the process of qualifying a witness as an expert and consists of asking the witness about his qualifications. Voir dire by the retaining attorney is followed by voir dire by all the other involved attorneys. After the witness is accepted by the court as an expert, then the retaining attorney begins his direct examination. The opposing attorney will then cross-examine the witness, asking the same sequence of questions, for the same purposes, as he would in a trial deposition. He may also have some new questions for the expert witness that were not asked in prior depositions.

When objections are raised by the attorneys in the courtroom, the judge will rule on them on the spot. If the objection is overruled, then the witness may proceed and answer the question. If the objection is sustained, then the witness should sit quietly and wait for the next question to be asked.

Each attorney takes his turn asking questions until each has no further questions. Then the witness is excused. When excused, he should leave the courtroom, not sit and further watch the trial (unless, of course, the retaining attorney has asked him to do so). That is the end of the forensic psychiatrist's participation in a case.

Opposing attorneys sometimes have a tendency to be argumentative with expert witnesses. It is important to avoid participating in such arguments. The opposing attorney's job is to reduce the credibility of the witness. If he can get the witness to argue with him in front of the jury, he succeeds in making the witness less credible.

If an attorney tells an expert witness to answer yes or no, but the question cannot be answered yes or no, it is fair for the expert to say so and avoid being pressured into giving a misleading answer.

If an attorney asks a question that contains incorrect information about the witness's prior testimony, it is fair to respond that the question mischaracterizes the previous testimony, the question contains incorrect information, or the question cannot be answered because it contains incorrect information. Some attorneys will allow the witness to explain what is incorrect about the question. Others will not allow such an explanation, but will instead quickly rephrase the question or ask a different question. An expert witness should avoid answering a question that contains incorrect information.

If an attorney asks a question that contradicts itself or is confusing in any other way, the witness should ask that the question be rephrased, or respond that the question is confusing. Answering a confusing question is likely to lead to further confusion.

It is wise to avoid joking on the witness stand. Jokes are based on something being out of proportion (He likes yogurt so much that he doesn't even have a refrigerator; he just leaves his central air conditioning set at 35 degrees) or out of place (This old movie projector is good for only one thing—an anchor). It is easy for jurors to misinterpret jokes or see them as irreverent or disrespectful. Jokes are out of place in the courtroom.

If an attorney is badgering or harassing a witness, the witness can turn to the judge and say, "Judge, I have answered this question the best that I can." Such a tactic is risky, however, and should be reserved for the worst instances. If the judge sides with the attorney, then the credibility of the witness is further reduced.

Ten

ETHICS OF
FORENSIC PSYCHIATRY

AMA's ETHICAL PRINCIPLES

Forensic psychiatrists are physicians first. The American Medical Association (AMA) has established principles of medical ethics applicable to all physicians.* These are the standards of conduct that define the essentials of honorable behavior for physicians:

1. A physician shall be dedicated to providing competent medical service with compassion and respect for human dignity.
2. A physician shall deal honestly with patients and colleagues, and strive to expose those physicians deficient in character or competence, or who engage in fraud or deception.
3. A physician shall respect the law and also recognize the responsibility to seek changes in those requirements which are contrary to the best interests of the patient.
4. A physician shall respect the rights of patients, of colleagues, and of other health professionals, and shall safeguard patient confidences within the constraints of the law.

*"Principles of Medical Ethics," from *Code of Medical Ethics: Current Opinions with Annotations* (p. xiv). © 1996, American Medical Association, Chicago. Reprinted with permission.

5. A physician shall continue to study, apply, and advance scientific knowledge, make relevant information available to patients, colleagues, and the public, obtain consultation, and use the talents of other health professionals when indicated.
6. A physician shall, in the provision of appropriate patient care, except in emergencies, be free to choose whom to serve, with whom to associate, and the environment in which to provide medical services.
7. A physician shall recognize a responsibility to participate in activities contributing to an improved community.

All physicians, including forensic psychiatrists, are held to these ethical principles. According to these principles, forensic psychiatrists are required to provide competent medical service with compassion and respect when examining forensic evaluees. Forensic psychiatrists are also required by these principles to respect the law and avoid fraud and deception.

APA's ETHICAL PRINCIPLES

The American Psychiatric Association (APA) has adopted and endorsed the AMA's *Principles of Medical Ethics.* All psychiatrists, including forensic psychiatrists, are held to the APA's ethical principles, both as psychiatrists and as physicians.

APPL's ETHICAL PRINCIPLES

The American Academy of Psychiatry and the Law (AAPL) has established ethical guidelines for forensic psychiatrists.* They are:

1. Preamble: The American Academy of Psychiatry and the Law is dedicated to the highest standards of practice in forensic psychiatry. Recognizing the unique aspects of this practice,

---

*Ethical guidelines for the practice of forensic psychiatry. In *AAPL Membership Directory* (pp. xi-xiv). © 1991, American Academy of Psychiatry and the Law, Bloomfield, CT. Reprinted with permission.

which is at the interface of the professions of psychiatry and the law, the Academy presents these guidelines for the ethical practice of forensic psychiatry.

2. Confidentiality: Respect for the individual's right of privacy and the maintenance of confidentiality are major concerns of the psychiatrist performing forensic evaluations. The psychiatrist maintains confidentiality to the extent possible given the legal context. Special attention is paid to any limitations on the usual precepts of medical confidentiality. An evaluation for forensic purposes begins with notice to the evaluee of any limitations on confidentiality. Information or reports derived from the forensic evaluation are subject to the rules of confidentiality as apply to the evaluation and any disclosure is restricted accordingly.

3. Consent: The informed consent of the subject of a forensic evaluation is obtained when possible. Where consent is not required, notice is given to the evaluee of the nature of the evaluation. If the evaluee is not competent to give consent, substituted consent is obtained in accordance with the laws of the jurisdiction.

4. Honesty and Striving for Objectivity: The forensic psychiatrist functions as an expert within the legal process. Although he may be retained by one party to a dispute in a civil matter, or the prosecution or defense in a criminal matter, he adheres to the principles of honesty and striving for objectivity. His clinical evaluation and the application of the data obtained to the legal criteria are performed in the spirit of such honesty and striving for objectivity. His opinion reflects this honesty and striving for objectivity.

5. Qualifications: Expertise in the practice of forensic psychiatry is claimed only in areas of actual knowledge and skills, training, and experience.

6. Procedures for Handling Complaints of Unethical Conduct: Complaints of unethical conduct against members of the Academy will be returned to the complainant with guidance as to where the complaint should be registered. Generally, they will be referred to the local district branch of the American Psychiatric Association (APA). If the member does not

belong to the APA, the complainant will be referred to the state licensing board or to the psychiatric association in the appropriate country. If either the APA, American Academy of Child and Adolescent Psychiatry, or the psychiatric association of another country should expel or suspend a member, AAPL will also expel or suspend the member upon notification of such action, regardless of continuing membership status in other organizations. AAPL will not necessarily follow the APA or other organizations in other actions.

BEING AN ADVOCATE

Attorneys are advocates for their clients. Forensic psychiatrists are advocates for their diagnoses and evaluation conclusions. It is unethical for a forensic psychiatrist to advocate for an evaluee. It is ethical for a forensic psychiatrist to (1) objectively evaluate a case, including an objective examination of the evaluee, (2) draw his conclusions with honesty and striving for objectivity, and then, after that point, (3) advocate for his conclusions. The ethical forensic psychiatrist will advocate for his conclusions, not for the person about whom the conclusions pertain.

BEING A DOUBLE AGENT

It is unethical for a forensic psychiatrist to be an agent for two different sides in a case. An example is a military psychiatrist evaluating both for the military and for the evaluee. The ethical forensic psychiatrist cannot ethically receive information from both sides (military and evaluee), draw conclusions for both sides, and then testify for both sides.

Also, it is unethical to receive information from one party in a case and then work, in any capacity, for another party in the case. If an ethical forensic psychiatrist receives any information beyond the name of a case from one party, then he should not receive any information from another party in the case, or participate in any way on behalf of another party, regarding that case.

CONSENT

It is unethical to examine an evaluee without his consent. The common exceptions to this principle are discussed in chapter 5.

EXPLANATION

Obviously, an examinee cannot give informed consent unless he knows to what he is consenting. The ethical forensic psychiatrist is obligated to explain to the examinee, before beginning an examination, (1) the identity of the examiner, (2) the purpose of the examination, and (3) the limits of confidentiality pertaining to the examination. Then, only after the examinee consents to be examined, is the ethical psychiatrist to examine the examinee.

The principle of informed consent does not apply when an examination is court ordered. Consent by a substitute consent giver (see page 49) should also be informed consent.

CONFIDENTIALITY

As just stated above, the ethical forensic psychiatrist is obligated to inform the examinee about the limits of the confidentiality of the examination findings. This is to occur before the start of the examination.

The ethical forensic psychiatrist is also obligated to keep confidential the information gained in any forensic case. The principles of confidentiality pertaining to the treatment of patients also apply to forensic cases. The ethical forensic psychiatrist will reveal information about a case only in accordance with the consent that has been given regarding release of information.

Eleven

Professional Liability Insurance

Necessity

Professional liability insurance is commonly called malpractice insurance. Most forensic psychiatrists do have professional liability insurance that covers them for both clinical work and forensic activities. If sued for malpractice, the insurance covers both the defense costs (attorney's fees) and the amount of money that must be paid to the plaintiff (settlement or award).

It is generally considered advisable to carry professional liability insurance. Some forensic specialists do not have such coverage, which is called "going bare." Although the likelihood of being sued for malpractice regarding forensic work is low, it does happen. The reasons for carrying coverage for forensic work are the same as for clinical work.

Types and Coverages

There are two types of professional liability insurance: occurrence and claims made.

Occurrence coverage is generally considered the preferred coverage. It covers liability for acts performed during a specified period of time, usually a year. Coverage is renewed annually. This insurance covers a claim no matter when it is made, even if made 20 years after the alleged act of malpractice. If a practitioner retires or takes a job that supplies malpractice coverage, then the policy can simply be cancelled for future coverage or not renewed. Occurrence coverage is generally more expensive than claims made coverage.

Claims made insurance covers liability for claims submitted during a specified period of time, usually a year. Coverage is renewed annually. This insurance covers claims made during the coverage period, regardless of when the alleged act of malpractice occurred. If a practitioner retires or takes a job that supplies malpractice coverage, then "tail coverage" is commonly purchased. The tail covers all claims made after the claims made coverage period ends. Although claims made coverage is generally less expensive than occurrence coverage, tail coverage is usually expensive, as much as five times the amount of the claims made annual premium. Tail coverage is purchased only once, when the physician does not continue his annual renewal of claims made coverage.

The amount of coverage purchased is the maximum amount that the insurance will pay in claims for each coverage period. For example, $100,000/$300,000 occurrence coverage means that the insurance company will pay up to $100,000 for any one claim, but no more than $300,000 in claims for any coverage period.

Commonly, defense costs, for attorney fees and other expenses, are in addition to these coverage limits. The insurance company will pay the defense costs in full, even if it pays the policy limit, in this case $100,000, to a claimant.

Tail coverage for claims made insurance has a hidden limit. If $100,000/$300,000 claims made coverage is in place for three years, then the insurance company will pay up to $300,000 *per year* in claims for the three covered years. If tail coverage is then purchased, the tail covers only a total of $300,000 for the entire length of the tail, which is the *entire future*, a period much longer than one year.

Most professional liability insurance policies will cover forensic activities as well as clinical activities. It is wise, however, to look for any such exception or limitation in any professional liability insurance policy.

If coverage is needed only for forensic work and not for clinical work, then professional liability insurance covering only forensic work can be purchased.

CARRIERS

Professional liability insurance companies are called carriers. Insurance policies are sold by insurance agents through insurance agencies.

Most carriers offer coverage only in some regions. The names and addresses of the regional carriers can commonly be obtained from a state medical society office or American Psychiatric Association district branch office.

There are three carriers that provide professional liability insurance for psychiatrists nationwide:

1. *Legion Insurance Company*
    Policy holder is the APA:
    Psychiatrists' Purchasing Group, Inc.
    1400 K Street NW
    Washington, DC 20005
    phone 202-682-1610
    Agent:
    Professional Risk Management Services, Inc.
    1000 Wilson Boulevard, Suite 2500
    Arlington, VA 22209-3901
    phone 703-907-3800 or 800-245-3333
    fax   703-276-0873

    This coverage is sponsored by the American Psychiatric Association and arranged by the Psychiatrist's Purchasing Group. APA membership is a prerequisite for purchasing this coverage.

2. *Frontier Insurance Company*
   Rock Hill, NY 12775-8000
   phone 914-796-2100
   National agent and program administrator:
   Medical Professional Liability Agency
   2 Depot Plaza
   Bedford Hills, NY 10507
   phone 914-666-0555 or 800-7MEDPRO
   fax   914-666-9319

   This individual coverage is also sold by regional agencies. This coverage is sponsored by the American Academy of Child and Adolescent Psychiatry. Membership in the Academy is not a prerequisite for purchasing this coverage. Coverage is not available in all states.

3. *The Medical Protective Company of Fort Wayne, Indiana*
   5814 Reed Road
   PO Box 15021
   Fort Wayne, IN 46885
   phone 219-485-9622

   This individual coverage is sold by regional agencies.

All three of these carriers offer policies that include coverage for forensic activities as well as clinical activities.

Complete Equity Markets, Inc. is the one agency that sells professional liability coverage without coverage for treating patients; the coverage is for "forensic litigation consultants." The coverage is offered nationwide (all products may not be available in all states, or may vary from state to state).

Complete Equity Markets, Inc.
1098 South Milwaukee Avenue
Wheeling, IL 60090-6398
phone 847-541-0900 or 800-323-6234
fax   847-541-0444

Twelve

ADVERTISING

NECESSITY

Advertising one's availability for forensic work is not necessary. Most forensic psychiatrists in private practice, however, prefer to be known and to have a referral base for forensic cases. Advertising is one way to build a referral base.

There was a time when advertising by a physician was considered to be unprofessional and unethical. This is no longer the case. As long as advertising is truthful, it is not considered unethical. Physician advertising is considered by some to be unprofessional. Such a judgment often depends upon the content, tone, claims, and character of the advertisement.

TARGET

The target for a forensic psychiatrist's advertising is referral sources, not the general public. The referral sources are attorneys (plaintiff, defense, prosecutor), insurance companies (workers' compensation, disability, automobile, product liability, malpractice, health, life), courts and judges, insurance adjusters, rehabilitation agencies, medical examiners, and others who have cases requiring forensic psychiatry input.

APPROACHES

Teaching

Because a forensic psychiatrist is first a physician, the form of advertising generally considered to be the most desirable is teaching. This can be done in the form of lectures at bar association meetings, teaching seminars at gatherings of judges, publication of professional papers and books, columns in bar association publications, or even offering educational programs to referral sources. The topics of such presentations can be, for example, specific areas of interest in forensic psychiatry, case presentations with appropriate safeguards for confidentiality, criteria for various diagnoses and findings, procedures used in forensic evaluations, or how psychiatric criteria are correlated to legal standards.

Volunteering

In the same way that a store might offer a free item in order to get a customer into the store, a forensic psychiatrist might offer to work on a few cases pro bono so that a law firm, prosecutor, public defender, or insurance company can see the quality and benefits of the forensic psychiatrist's involvement.

A way of partially volunteering is to work for agencies or courts that pay less than the usual forensic psychiatry fees. A forensic psychiatrist might offer to work at reduced or limited fees for a court, a prosecutor, a court appointed attorney, or a public defender's office.

Print Advertising

Print advertising can be used to make one's availability and credentials known; examples include direct mail advertising and a classified or display ad in a bar association newsletter.

Directories

Many directories of expert witnesses exist, which list all sorts of forensic experts, such as ballistics experts, engineers, documents examiners, etc. For a fee, a forensic expert or an attorney can have his name listed as an available resource. Credentials and other information about the expert might also be included in the listing. Commonly, such listings cost an annual fee, just like a listing in the yellow pages of the telephone book. This form of advertising is generally considered a waste of money for forensic psychiatrists. It is generally felt that an attorney will not select a forensic psychiatrist from such a directory.

Litigation Expert Agencies

There are many agencies for litigation experts. These agencies gather lists of forensic psychiatrists and all sorts of litigation experts. An attorney who needs an expert contracts with the agency, who puts the attorney in touch with an expert. The attorney pays the agency, and the agency then pays the expert. Such agencies sometimes have a reputation for providing experts who are "hired guns," experts who will testify whatever the attorney wishes, regardless of the truth. Working for an agency is not considered unethical. Testifying whatever the attorney wishes, however, regardless of the truth, *is* unethical.

Because of the negative reputation of such agencies in general, being associated with them can be more of a liability than an asset to one's credibility.

News Commentators

One can volunteer to be available to radio and television stations or newspapers to comment on the forensic psychiatry aspects of news stories. This does get one's name known in the community as a psychiatrist who is knowledgeable about such issues. This can lead to referrals of other cases. It is common for a television news department to interview a mental health expert, for example, when a heinous crime occurs, and the community is upset and wondering why a person would do such a thing. While making diagnoses in such situations is unethical, it is ethical to educate the public about psychiatric principles in general.

Talk Shows

Forensic psychiatrists who have volunteered to participate in radio or television talk shows have found success in generating referrals of clinical cases. They have not found, however, that such advertising generates much in the way of forensic work.

Membership and Participation in Medical Societies

Referrals can come from medical, psychiatric, or forensic psychiatry societies, and from the local, county, regional, state, or national levels of those societies. Examples of such societies are the city or county medical society, the state medical society, the American Psychiatric Association (APA) district branch, or the American Academy of Psychiatry and the Law (AAPL).

When a society gets a call from, for example, an attorney who is looking for a forensic psychiatrist, the society will give the attorney only the names of members of the society. Joining the various medical societies is a way to receive such referrals.

Participating in the activities of medical societies, such as serving on committees or becoming an officer, increases the likelihood of being referred any inquiries that come to the society.

Active involvement in particular activities can directly create referral networks. For example, if a forensic psychiatrist is on a local medical society committee of liaison with the local bar association, that psychiatrist can develop and participate in programs presented by the medical society to the bar association. This is a way to quickly become known to the local attorneys.

Social Settings

The more known a person and his particular interests are, the more likely others will think of him when they need a person with that particular interest. A person is more likely to call a dentist he has met at the country club than a dentist he has never met.

Socializing in any setting is a process of enabling others to know one's particular interests. A forensic psychiatrist can introduce himself and be known as a physician, a psychiatrist, or a forensic psychiatrist. The more people who know one as a forensic psychiatrist, the greater the likelihood that forensic cases will be referred to that psychiatrist.

The more people one knows, the more likely referrals will come his way. Also, the more people who know the psychiatrist, the more likely referrals will come his way. By doing public, community, or church work, being active in neighborhoods, condominium associations, schools, Parent Teacher Organizations (PTOs), community organizations, charity organizations, and other such groups, a forensic psychiatrist can become known by a wide range of people.

BOARD CERTIFICATION

Board certification in forensic psychiatry is not necessary, but it is a helpful credential when establishing credibility. A board certification is an objective indicator of a physician's fulfilling a professional standard.

BOARDS

Until 1994, the American Board of Forensic Psychiatry was the usual certifying body in forensic psychiatry. That board no longer offers certification. That function was taken over by the American Board of Psychiatry and Neurology, which began certifying Added Qualifications in Forensic Psychiatry in 1995.

The Added Qualifications certification is valid for 10 years. Then the psychiatrist must pass the certification test again, to be certified for another 10 years.

In order to take the Added Qualifications examination, a person must be board certified in general psychiatry. Beginning in 2000, a board certified psychiatrist will be required to have completed a fellowship accredited by the Accreditation Council for Graduate Medical Education (ACGME) in order to be eligible to take the

Added Qualifications examination. The ACGME began accrediting fellowship programs in 1997. Thus, starting in 2000, the only psychiatrists who may take the added qualifications examination are the board certified psychiatrists who completed an accredited forensic fellowship after 1996.

One-year fellowships are available in forensic psychiatry. They are viewed as a fifth year of psychiatry residency. A fellowship is not required or necessary. However, the more training and credentials an expert witness has, the more credible his testimony. A list of fellowship positions is available from AAPL (address below).

The American Board of Forensic Psychiatry can be accessed through the American Academy of Psychiatry and the Law (AAPL; address is listed below). Forensic psychiatrists who are certified by this board may refer inquirers to this board for verification of their board certification status. Certification by the American Board of Forensic Psychiatry is not time limited.

Applications for the examination for Added Qualifications in Forensic Psychiatry are available from

American Board of Psychiatry and Neurology
500 Lake Cook Road, Suite 335
Deerfield, IL 60015
phone   708-945-7900

Board certification is also available from the American College of Forensic Examiners. For a membership fee of $100 and a list of experience in the forensic psychiatry field, a psychiatrist can receive board certification as a Forensic Examiner and become a Diplomate of the American Board of Forensic Examiners. For those who do not qualify by virtue of experience, a written examination can be completed at home. Board certification in general psychiatry is not required. Applications are available from

The American College of Forensic Examiners
2750 East Sunshine
PO Box 4006
Springfield, MO 65808-4006

phone   417-881-3818 or 800-423-9737
fax   417-881-4702
website http://www.acfe.com

Board certification by the American Board of Forensic Psychiatry, or Added Qualification in Forensic Psychiatry from the American Board of Psychiatry and Neurology, are commonly considered to be more desirable and credible than certification by the American College of Forensic Examiners.

BOARD REVIEW COURSES

There are two forensic psychiatry board review courses available. The more popular one is offered through the American Academy of Psychiatry and the Law (AAPL). This course is chaired by Phillip Resnick, M.D., of Case Western Reserve Medical School in Cleveland, Ohio. It is always offered during the three days prior to the annual AAPL meeting in October, in the same location as the AAPL meeting. It is occasionally offered at other times and locations. Information and registration materials are available from

American Academy of Psychiatry and the Law (AAPL)
One Regency Drive
PO Box 30
Bloomfield, CT 06002-0030
phone   860-242-5450 or 800-331-1389
fax   860-286-0787*

*AAPL also offers resource materials, such as a compilation of landmark cases, through its Resource Center, at the same address. The landmark cases in forensic psychiatry are the cases that have created the standards and shaped the laws. The board certification tests commonly focus heavily on the landmark cases. It is wise to be familiar with them before attempting to pass a board certification test.

The other board review course is offered by the Osler Institute. It is offered one or two times per year, usually in Chicago, but occasionally other places. Information and registration materials are available from

The Osler Institute
1094 East Dawn Drive
PO Box 2218
Terre Haute, IN 47802-9971
phone   812-299-5658 or 800-356-7537

Although not considered a board review course, National Training Conferences are occasionally held by the American College of Forensic Examiners (address above).

FORENSIC PSYCHIATRIC ORGANIZATIONS

Membership in forensic psychiatric organizations is not required or essential, but it is helpful in many ways.

1. *Education* The organizations hold meetings, both nationally and regionally. The meetings commonly have themes. The larger meetings offer mini-courses, similar to those at the APA Annual Meeting, on various aspects of forensic psychiatry. In addition to being a place to learn, the meetings are also a place to teach.

AAPL has an annual meeting each October for 3 ½ days. AAPL also maintains a resource center of educational materials available to members and to the general public.

2. *Collegiality* Psychiatry is a medical specialty, and forensic psychiatry is a medical subspecialty, in which much time is spent out of contact with colleagues. Organizational meetings are opportunities to meet other forensic psychiatrists, to exchange ideas and experiences, and to discuss issues.

3. *Referrals* Attending meetings is a way to get to know others in the field, particularly the special interests that each colleague has, for referring cases to each other. The organizations are also a source of referrals of cases. When the organization gets an inquiry looking for a forensic psychiatrist, it refers the inquirer to the appropriate members, considering location and particular areas of expertise.

4. *Standards and ethics*   The organizations establish the standards of the profession. For example, AAPL has established standards for testifying about a person whom the forensic psychiatrist has not examined. They also establish ethical principles for the profession. The ethics of the AMA, the APA, and AAPL are presented in chapter 10.

5. *Debate*   Forensic psychiatric organizations are also the forum for complaints, problems, debates, and discussions of issues. AAPL works to identify issues and take positions on them. Even if an issue is not clarified by an organization, it is the place to talk to colleagues who hold various positions on the various issues.

ORGANIZATIONS

American Medical Association (AMA)
535 North Dearborn Street
Chicago, IL 60610
phone   312-464-5000 or 800-262-3211

American Psychiatric Association (APA)
1400 K Street, NW
Washington, DC 20005
phone   202-682-6000
fax   202-682-6114

The AMA has state and local chapters; the APA has regional chapters. Both organizations hold national and regional meetings, publish a multitude of books, journals, and pamphlets, lobby in Washington, and provide a host of services for members.

American Academy of Psychiatry and the Law (AAPL)
One Regency Drive
PO Box 30
Bloomfield, CT 06002-0030
phone   860-242-5450 or 800-331-1389
fax   860-286-0787

The AAPL has regional chapters. Some are large, such as the midwest chapter, which covers 13 states. Others are small, such as the tristate chapter covering the New York City metropolitan area. For example, the midwest chapter has an annual meeting each spring for 1½ days. The tristate chapter has meetings that last a few hours. It also has year-long courses. AAPL publishes a quarterly journal and a newsletter three times a year. The AAPL Resource Center makes materials available to both members and nonmembers.

American College of Forensic Examiners
2750 East Sunshine
PO Box 4006
Springfield, MO 65808-4006
phone   417-881-3818 or 800-423-9737
fax   417-881-4702

The College publishes a journal every two months, offers certification and diplomate designation, and holds meetings periodically.

American College of Forensic Psychiatry
PO Box 5870
Balboa Island, CA 92662
phone   714-831-0236
fax   714-673-7710

The American College of Forensic Psychiatry publishes a journal and holds periodic meetings.

American Academy of Forensic Sciences
PO Box 669
Colorado Springs CO 80901
phone 719-636-1100

The American Academy of Forensic Sciences is a reputable organization encompassing highly varied areas of forensic interest. It holds annual meetings and publishes a journal.

SUGGESTED READINGS

Appelbaum, P. S., & Gutheil, T. G. (1991). *Clinical handbook of psychiatry and the law.* Baltimore: Williams & Wilkins.

Melton, G. B., Poythress, N. G., & Slobogin, C. (1987). *Psychological evaluations for the courts: A handbook for mental health professionals and lawyers.* New York: Guilford.

Rosner, R. (1994). *Principles and practice of forensic psychiatry.* New York: Chapman & Hall.

Schetky, D., & Benedek, E. (1992). *Clinical handbook of child psychiatry and the law.* Baltimore: Williams & Wilkins.

Simon, R. I. (1992). *Clinical psychiatry and the law.* Washington, DC: American Psychiatric Press.

SAMPLE REPORTS

CRIMINAL DEFENSE CASE: GEORGE GUNNER

STEVEN H. BERGER, M.D.
Diplomate, American Board of Psychiatry and Neurology
Diplomate, American Board of Forensic Psychiatry

825 Apple Road, SE   Atlanta, GA 12345-6789
Phone: 616-957-0850   Fax: 616-957-3045

January 1, 1999

Dennis Defense
Attorney at Law
Smith, Jones, and Defense
123 Main Street
Atlanta, Georgia 12345-6789

Re: George G. Gunner

CONFIDENTIAL PSYCHIATRIC REPORT

Dear Mr. Defense:

At your request, I performed a psychiatric evaluation of the case of above named subject, George G. Gunner. As part of that evaluation, I examined him in my office on December 31, 1998.

For your reference, a copy of my current curriculum vitae is attached.

Prior to my examination of the subject, I reviewed the several documents that you sent. They are:

1. School records regarding the subject from kindergarten to mid-twelfth grade in the St. Louis School System.
2. Treatment records of St. Louis psychiatrist Alice A. Apple, M.D., regarding the subject from age 4 to age 8.
3. Psychological testing conducted by St. Louis psychologist Burton B. Baxter, Ph.D., regarding the subject at age 10.
4. Treatment records from Parker Psychiatric Hospital in St. Louis regarding the subject from January 31, 1990, to March 31, 1990.
5. Treatment records from Parchment Psychiatric Hospital in St. Louis regarding the subject from November 13, 1990, to December 13, 1990.
6. School records regarding the subject from Atlanta City Center Community College in Atlanta from age 18 to age 20.
7. Summary of Criminal Charges and Convictions (rap sheet) from the Georgia State Police regarding the subject, ending with October 1, 1998.
8. The report of your private investigator, dated November 1, 1998.
9. The records of the subject's general doctor, Dennis D. Dunham, M.D., of St. Louis, covering the subject from age 2 to the present.

I used the content of these documents to prepare for myself a list of questions to ask the subject. I did not rely upon the content of these documents in reaching my conclusions regarding this case.

The purpose of this evaluation is to determine whether the subject, George Gunner, (1) is competent to stand trial at this time and (2) fulfills the criteria of legal insanity regarding the charges against him for his actions on November 1, 1997. The charges are (1) attempted murder, (2) unlawful possession of a firearm, and (3) conspiracy to commit murder.

At the beginning of my examination of him, I explained to the subject the purpose of the examination and the absence of the usual medical confidentiality. I explained to him that I will be releasing my report of this examination to his attorney. I explained to him that I may be required to testify in a deposition or trial and reveal the information that he provides to me. He agreed to participate in the examination with this understanding.

The following are my findings and conclusions regarding my evaluation of this subject.

HISTORY OF SITUATION

The following is the history of the situation in question, as told to me by the subject.

The subject is age 20. He is charged with (1) attempted murder, (2) unlawful possession of a firearm, and (3) conspiracy to commit murder.

The story of the charges began at age 7. The subject attended the Elwood Edmonds Elementary School in St. Louis. At age 12, he switched to the Benjamin Rush School in St. Louis, a school that specialized in learning disabilities. He was doing poorly at the Edmonds school. Educational and psychological testing in sixth grade had revealed that he had problems in tracking, nonverbal communication, and short-term memory. Due to these findings, it was suggested that he transfer to the Benjamin Rush School. In the process of trying to fit in at the Rush School, he started acting up.

The subject's acting up consisted of making stupid noises and being a smart-ass. He was, in general, a jerk. The acting up was not personal against the teachers. He liked the teachers. "But it just wasn't cool to like the teachers, so I acted like I didn't." Sometimes he would get in shouting matches with teachers at the Rush School. On one occasion, he even shoved a teacher.

His acting up worked. He felt that he fit in at the Rush School. Things went smoothly for him from seventh grade to tenth grade. He maintained a very delicate balance between acting up so as to be like the other students, but not going too far and causing big problems. In eleventh grade at the Rush School, however, he went too far. He got in fights all the time. He would kick the waste baskets across the room. He would knock over other students' desks. "I never, ever found out why I did that stuff."

The subject would black out and do violent acts. It was not as if he didn't remember it. It was as if it happened somewhere else, or as if it was a movie and not real.

In addition to perpetrating violent behavior, the subject would, at times, get kicked or punched, but it never hurt. He was never mad at the people he would fight. He was in vicious fights, but he was never angry at the other people. He would feel angry before the fight, but not during the fight. "I guess I never really realized that I wasn't really angry at the person while I was fighting them. I guess I never really thought about it until now."

Until tenth grade at the Rush School, the subject had friends, but by January of his eleventh-grade year, he had lost all his friends at the school.

Until age 11, the subject had never encountered people different from himself. The Rush School, however, had people from every neighborhood in the city. Almost all the students in the Rush School were poor or from broken families. The subject came from a family of means, and his family was intact.

In tenth grade, the subject would go to downtown St. Louis to skateboard in the parking ramps with a friend of his. In downtown St. Louis, the subject hooked up with a social group called the St. Louis Longhairs. The first time he encountered them, he came out of a McDonald's restaurant with his skateboarding friend, and found about 15 Longhairs mulling around the sidewalk. He had never seen such people before. They were always walking around the sidewalks of the downtown. The subject did not go downtown in order to meet the Longhairs.

His second time downtown, the subject ended up talking with three of the Longhairs on his way home from skateboarding, as he was walking to the bus stop. They told him that the Longhairs hang out between 3rd and 4th Streets on Division Avenue. "They were just a bunch of scary guys who seemed to like me and seemed to look out for me."

The Longhairs befriended the subject. Also, he sought them out. He would try to fit in with them. "If I could fit in with them, things at my school would go a lot easier. If a gang member at school gave me sass, I could just sick the Longhairs on them." The subject never needed to send the Longhairs after the gang members at school, however. The gang members were at the Rush School.

The subject never discussed politics with the Longhairs. Mostly, the Longhairs just drank and complained about the government doing too little for the people.

When the subject was in tenth grade, the family moved to Rockland, a suburb about 20 miles west of St. Louis. Rush School was in the northern part of St. Louis. The subject's mother still worked as a teacher on the south side of St. Louis. His mother drove him to the downtown bus transfer station each morning on her way to work, and picked him up there each day on her way home from work. So the subject was in downtown St. Louis twice each day, with time waiting for his rides.

While he was in eleventh grade at the Rush School, the subject's mother picked him up in the afternoon at the school, because she worked only in the morning. But in twelfth grade, he would take the bus from school to downtown, where his mother would pick him up. She was working full-time that year.

Starting at age 16, in eleventh grade, he would run away for three to five days at a time. The last day of eleventh grade, he ran away for five days with his girlfriend. When he returned, he had a partly shaven head and the remainder of his hair was green. He was a Longhair. His girlfriend came to his parents' house in Rockland with him. The subject found that he felt out of place there, at home.

Then the subject moved with his family and his girlfriend three years ago, in the fourth month of his twelfth-grade year, to Atlanta, Georgia. The St. Louis Longhairs called the Atlanta Longhairs to make sure that the subject stayed involved with the organization. He really did not want to continue with the organization here in Atlanta, but he had no choice.

Finally, in an attempt to change things, the subject broke up with his girlfriend and admitted himself to the psychiatric unit of Middleton Hospital in Atlanta in December, 1995. He was there for about five weeks. His treating psychiatrist was Harold Harvest, M.D. He was discharged in time to start the second semester of his senior year at Jefferson High School in Atlanta.

About three weeks into the second semester of his senior year, the subject was introduced to Kris, a member of Righteous S.S., which is the same as the German S.S. from World War II. The subject ended up becoming friends with a friend of Kris named Jack. Jack is a codefendant in the charges against the subject.

With Jack, the subject would drink, use drugs, hang out, go to the bars, go to the beaches, and do similar things. The subject and Jack remained friends for a few months, with no significant events. They didn't talk much about politics over the years.

A significant event then occurred in August, 1997, in the summer after the subject had returned from Italy. Jack encouraged the subject to purchase an assault rifle, an SKS. The subject had always wanted to be in the military. He was impressed when Jack showed the subject the similar gun that Jack had bought. The subject then bought the assault rifle. He purchased it then because it was about to be banned, and he wanted to get one before they became unavailable. He also purchased other military items at that time.

Jack would not order the subject to do such things. He would simply state, "You are doing this." In this way Jack often told the subject what to do.

At the time the subject bought the gun, Jack started to talk to the subject about political issues, such as the changing government policies and the approaching ban on assault weapons.

The subject did not plan to use the rifle. He felt that he and Jack were like a two-man militia that would be prepared in case of invasion or something. "It seems pretty silly now. I don't know why I went for any of this stuff."

"To me, it all seemed like a game still. Nothing serious." Jack owned two rifles and two handguns. He also had ammunition for all the guns. The two handguns were unregistered. Jack said that he was following orders from the leader of the Righteous S.S. group in New York. Jack said he was directed to get 2,000 rounds per gun.

About a year ago, Jack introduced the subject to Sam. Then, in Autumn, 1997, the subject ran into Sam at Atlanta City Center Community College. Jack, Sam, and the subject then began to hang out with each other. They would go drinking, but the subject does not drink much. He handles beer the best, and might drink as much as 44 ounces of beer in a day. If he drinks hard liquor, the subject passes out with his eyes open and does not know what happens.

If the subject smokes marijuana, he does not allow himself to drive because his driving is erratic under the influence of marijuana. For example, he will see a stoplight, but not register in his mind that it means he must stop. If he smokes marijuana and drinks beer, the effect of the marijuana is enhanced.

On about October 27, 1997, a Thursday evening, the subject went to Tony's house. Tony was a friend of Jack's. Sam was already there. Sam had already drunk a lot and was drunk. Jack was there also and had already drunk some beer. The subject, at Tony's house, drank the beer he had brought with him. They also smoked marijuana.

At Tony's house, after Tony left to go to the store, Sam and Jack got into an argument and Sam left the room. While Sam was walking out, Jack took an unloaded pistol out of his pocket and pointed it at Sam's back. Jack pulled the trigger a couple times. Sam didn't know this happened. Jack looked at the subject, kind of laughed, and said, "Wasn't that funny?" The subject just looked at Jack and gave no other response.

After Tony had been gone about an hour, Jack, Sam, and the subject left the house. They got in the car and started to drive away. Jack asked if the subject had his magazine, *Shotgun News*, with him. He did not. Jack ran back into the house to get the magazine. When he came out with the magazine, he got back into the car and tossed the magazine into the back seat.

The subject was driving as they started to drive away. Sam, looking out the back window from the back seat, saw three or four black men walking toward the rear of the car, in the middle of the street. The black men were dressed in black. One of the black men was reaching in his belt, as if reaching for a gun. The subject then saw Jack lean out the front passenger window. He then heard about seven shots coming from what appeared to be Jack's pistol. Then the subject drove away as fast as he could, even before Jack was fully back in the car.

Driving away, they passed police cars going to the scene of the shooting. The subject was very nervous. Jack told the subject to relax. The subject was scared, "It was the first time that anything like that had happened to me. I had never been close to a gun being fired before, except at the FBI building in Washington, on their tour."

The following day was Tuesday, November 1, 1997. That was the next day the subject had classes at the community college. At school, the subject ran into Sam. The subject told Sam, as they were having lunch together, that he was nervous about the shooting incident, and that he did not want it to happen again. The subject and Sam planned to go to a movie that evening with Jack. They planned to see *Pulp Fiction*.

That evening, the subject picked up Sam and Jack. They stopped at a store and bought a bottle of Canadian Mist whiskey. They were early for the movie, so they stopped at Ken's house. Ken was another friend of Jack's. Jack and Sam drank the whiskey at Ken's house. Someone lit a pipe of marijuana and passed it around. The subject, along with the others, smoked the marijuana. After becoming disinhibited, and with the prompting of the others, the subject did drink some of the whiskey. They challenged him to drink half a glass of the whiskey straight. He met the challenge and did so. He also drank more whiskey. He is not sure how many more half glasses he drank, but he knows it was more than three.

When it was too late to go to the movie, the three of them went to John's house to play cards. John was another friend of Jack's. The subject loaned Sam some money because Sam had no money with which to bet in the card game. The subject watched as the others played cards. Someone poured the subject a large glass of beer, which he sipped as he watched. Jack and Sam were cheating at the card game. They both lost, despite their cheating.

"The next thing I remember, Jack and Sam were arguing with each other." Sam poured his beer on Jack. Jack threw his drink at Sam, but missed, and broke a lamp instead. They were about to punch and kick each other, but the fight was broken up. Finally they apologized to eachother. Jack said he was whiskey bent, which means drunk, mean, and angry. Jack said that, because he was whiskey bent, he wanted to go out and do something.

When the subject drives under the influence of alcohol, it feels as if he has not been drinking. At such times, however, he must concentrate entirely on his driving, without even so much as talking. He feels he can safely drive under the influence, however, "I might swerve a little bit, but it's not outside the lane."

The three of them got in the subject's parents' car, with the subject driving, and drove away. None of them had any business being on the road. "I shouldn't have been driving, but there was no one else I could really give up the keys to."

As they were driving, Jack pulled out his pistol with the clip in it, and handed it to the subject. It was loaded. The subject had his window open about four inches because he was smoking a cigarette. He put the gun between his legs on the seat. Jack was telling the subject where to drive. One place they passed was Jack's place of employment at the corner of Maple and Elm Streets.

On a side street, they saw a black man dressed like the three or four black men from the first shooting incident. "Jack told me to turn around, so I drove around the block." Jack told the subject to get him, or shoot him, or something. The subject pulled the car over to the curb. Jack yelled at the subject to shoot the black man. The subject held the gun out the window and tried to shoot the gun, but it would not work. The subject pulled the gun back in the car, found the gun's safety on, and disarmed the safety. Jack yelled at the subject again to shoot the man. He again held the gun outside the window. The subject knew that he did not really want to shoot the man. Jack again yelled at the subject to shoot the man. The subject pulled the trigger once, knowing the shot was aimed to miss the man.

Then the subject pulled the gun back in the car again. Then Jack yelled to the subject that he missed the man and to shoot the man again. The subject held the gun outside again and shot two shots in front of the man. He then put the gun back inside the car and drove away, south on Elm. As they were driving away, the inside of the car smelled like meth, a drug that the subject once used.

As they were driving, the subject dropped Sam off first. On the way to Sam's house, Jack was saying that they had to kill Tony two days later because Tony was more interested in his musical band than in the Righteous S.S. organization. The subject dropped off Sam, then Jack. Then he went home and went to sleep. He did not vomit that night upon lying down. His usual pattern was to vomit upon lying down, after drinking.

The next day, the subject remembered the shooting as if it was a bad dream that didn't really happen. "It was a not big deal. It was like a regular day."

The next day, Thursday, Sam was not at school, which the subject thought was strange. The subject was looking for Sam. He wanted to tell Sam that the shooting and similar activities had to stop. The subject decided that he was not going to call Jack that evening. He did not want to have to deal with Jack and Sam. He did not want to spend a lot of time with Jack.

The subject normally had an appointment with Dr. Kandu, the subject's treating psychiatrist, every Thursday. The Thursday after the second shooting incident, Dr. Kandu was on vacation, so the subject did not have his usual Thursday appointment that day. The subject really wanted to talk to Dr. Kandu, but had already decided that he would not see Jack until after he next saw Dr. Kandu. The subject was scheduled to see Dr. Kandu nine days after the second shooting incident. As it turned out, the subject was in jail. He was arrested seven days after the second shooting incident.

At this point, the subject is still scared that the Righteous S.S. people in New York will cause problems for him. He wishes he knew who the people in New York are, so that he could inform the police about them.

The Atlanta chapter of the New York Righteous S.S. organization is called Das Reich. The subject does not know what Das

Reich means. He knows that the German Nazi organization was called the Third Reich. By the time the subject was age 19, he could not distance himself from the organization without being in danger of them killing him, blowing up his car, or such actions.

There are several people named Sam in the subject's story. Sam Ash is the Sam who was with the subject at the time of both shootings.

The subject has thought a lot about the alternative actions he could have taken, as opposed to shooting the black man. If he refused to follow Jack's order to shoot, the subject felt that he would then be at risk for being shot, on the spot by Jack, or later by the people from New York. He made the choice that he felt was the most right, or the least wrong, to shoot and miss the man. "Shooting and missing I thought was the safest for everyone."

"I haven't even considered that I'm more than likely going to spend some time in jail or prison for this."

The subject feels he was on automatic at the time he shot at the man, the same way he drives his car when under the influence of alcohol. "That night, I was being piloted, led by the nose."

The police originally wanted the subject to come to the police station and answer questions about a couple shootings in which the subject was involved. He responded, "What?" as if it didn't happen, or as if he is keeping himself from feeling anything about the incident in question.

For the week following the second shooting, he was able to get himself to believe that the shooting had not occurred. He could even deny any knowledge of the shootings without raising his blood pressure or pulse.

But by the time the police called the subject for questioning, the subject and his car were identified by the victim, and Sam had told the police about the subject's involvement.

The subject thought he missed the victim. As it turns out, one bullet grazed the victim. The subject reasons that the bullet that hit

George Gunner
January 1, 1999
page 13

the victim must have ricocheted off another object before hitting the man.

The subject never gave much thought about the political aspects of the Longhairs. He hung around them at age 15 because he thought they were cool. When he no longer needed to align himself with the Longhairs, he was unable to disassociate himself from them. Ironically, he can now disassociate himself from the Longhairs.

At this point, the subject is not mad at Sam. "And I certainly don't have any anger toward Isaac Ingham (the victim), whatever his name is." The subject would like to tell Ingham that he would do anything he could to help him.

In all honesty, the subject does not think that there is a connection between the organization in New York and the organization in Atlanta.

The subject feels that, "You are who you hang out with." He didn't know this until just the last week or so, when he began thinking about this. The subject always thought, while he was with Jack, that he was his own person. Now, in retrospect, he sees that he became very much like Jack. He now sees that he even laughed like Jack laughs. He thought his sister and his mother didn't know what they were talking about when they advised him to be careful in associating with Jack.

In the summer of 1997, the subject was working about 60 hours a week and didn't see Jack. Then, at the end of the summer, he did get back together with Jack, and their association resumed. But Jack was different by that time. The subject feels that Jack was changed due to the death of his father and the birth of his child. They were celebrating the birth of Jack's child on the night of the first shooting.

The subject got into this legal problem "by talking the talk and being forced to walk the walk." The subject was hanging out with a group of people with whom shooting blacks was acceptable. But such behavior is not acceptable to the subject. However, in order to be accepted by the group, the subject verbally agreed that he would shoot blacks, even though the subject would not do such a thing. When he found himself in the situation in which he shot at Ingham, he actually pulled the trigger 1% to save face with Jack and Sam, and 99% to avoid being killed by the Righteous S.S.

The subject felt that, if he had not pulled the trigger, as Jack directed, Jack or his friends, perhaps the people from New York, would have killed or maimed the subject within a week. Today, he is still afraid of being killed by Jack's people. This is one of the reasons the subject is content to stay at home at this point and leave his house only with his mother.

The following is the history of this case, as told to me by the subject's mother, Gladys Gunner, on December 31, 1997.

The subject is indiscriminate about the things he tells people. He is worse than a blabbermouth. He talks on and on to strangers or anyone about all details that are no one's business. One example is, at about age 3, the subject introduced his mother to the sales clerk at a carpet store, and included that his father's name for the mother is Honey.

The mother feels that the subject's whole life has been a walk along a balance beam. The subject falls off the balance beam periodically, and the mother then obtains a psychological evaluation, psychological treatment, or some sort of help to get him back on the beam.

Even in kindergarten, the teacher noticed that the subject is a follower. He never initiates any idea on his own. At home, even now at age 20, he never brushes his teeth or showers daily, unless the mother reminds him each time.

The subject seems to have no routine in his life. There isn't anything that he does everyday without prompting from the mother. He will follow the mother around the house in the morning, dressed in his robe, telling her things that are unimportant, until she tells him to go and get dressed.

Bundled instructions are useless for the subject. He must be told each step in succession, after the previous step is done. If he is told to straighten his room, he will go there with the intention of straightening his room, but he will end up lying on his bed listening to music. He has a list of steps he must follow to straighten his room, but he does not look at the list unless he is reminded to look at it. Two steps are too much. He can follow only one step at a time.

The subject is never defiant. He is eager to please others. He seems happy, like a puppy with a wagging tail, when he pleases others.

The subject is never aggressive toward people. He has never hit his sister, Ginger, who is 2 years, 8 months younger. The most aggressive thing he ever did to her was to hold her ankles when she would try to crawl, or remove her fingers when she, as a toddler, would grab things to pull herself up to standing.

Once, at about age 10, the subject was angry. He had just returned to St. Louis from living with his grandmother in Milwaukee, Wisconsin, for about six months. He took a swing at his mother and missed her. That was the only time he ever tried to hit her. There were other times at about age 10 when he threw a rollerskate against a door, he threw his alarm clock against a wall, and he threw his camera. The subject had a verbally abusive teacher that year, for the second half of the school year.

The subject has never had the strength that other people have to stand up to things that are wrong or hurtful.

In fourth grade when the subject was unable to copy things from the blackboard, the teacher treated him as if he were simply refusing to copy the material. She would then punish the subject by, for example, having him sit under her desk for a while.

The mother has noticed that punishment seems to have no

effect on the subject. It is not successful in changing his behavior. The mother never spanked the subject or his sister. If she told him to sit on a chair for 10 minutes, he would, as long as she stayed in the room with him. While sitting there, he would try to charm the mother and entice her to talk to him and to not stop her love for him. When the mother is troubled, her pattern is to withdraw.

If, during a punishment, the mother told the subject to stop talking for 10 minutes, he could not stop his talking. If she would leave the room, he would follow her, failing to stay on the chair. At this point, at age 20, he still cannot stop talking to her when she tells him to stop.

The subject was never punished by being sent to his room because it did not work. He has always been very good at distracting himself. If he were sent to his room, he would distract himself with his books or music and forget that he was being punished.

When the subject was young, the mother had building blocks, dress-up clothes, and art materials as toys for him. She was very careful to provide healthy toys for him.

The subject's fifth grade teacher noticed that the subject could not stay in his chair. She finally required that he keep contact with his desk, as if on a tether. She also noticed that he was unable to pay attention in the classroom.

In sixth grade, the subject was expected to work out of a locker, which he could not do. Finally, the guidance counselor arranged for the subject to have a desk in her office. She would meet him there between each classroom hour and help him get the materials he needed to take to the next hour's class.

Sixth grade was the first time the mother noticed that the subject was a victim. The other kids would pick on him at the bus stop. The mother noticed that the subject did not seem to comprehend that he was posturing himself as a victim. The mother tried to teach the subject how to walk with authority, so he would not look like a victim, but, "It was hopeless." She found it impossible for him to learn to walk with authority. To deal with the bus stop problem, the mother organized a car pool with some of the other mothers who were similarly upset by the bus stop problem.

When the subject wanted something expensive and it was not provided, he felt deprived. But some of the things he wanted were unreasonable. One example was a $200 skateboard when the subject was in fourth grade. Finally, the subject bought a used skateboard for $25. But it was stolen before the schoolyear ended.

As time passed, the subject chose to spend his time with younger children. They would not victimize him or take advantage of him. The parents of the younger children said that their children idolized the subject. The parents loved the subject. They considered the subject to be a role model for their children. The younger children would ask the subject to help them play baseball. He could pitch so that the younger children could play the other positions and have a game.

The subject would play an elaborate game of hide and seek with the younger children.

In St. Louis, the subject's closest friend was a boy one year younger. That boy is now a junior at Stanford in physics. He had ulcerative colitis and Crohn's disease. The subject visited the boy on alternate days when the boy was in the hospital for a protracted period of time. Then, when the subject was in Parchment Hospital, the boy visited the subject. The boy's parents adored the subject.

The mother first noticed about three years ago that others were taking advantage of the subject. Whenever anyone needed a ride, they would call the subject. Whether the subject was interested in the activity for which the ride was needed was irrelevant. The friends would call at outrageous hours and make unreasonable requests, but the subject would still provide the ride. The phone calls from the friends would, of course, awaken the household.

George Gunner
January 1, 1999
page 18

The subject never refused to give a ride to a caller.

When the mother limits the subject, telling him that he may not do something, he slams doors, stomps off to his room, and says things such as, "I know you're right, Mother, but I don't want you to be right." Then he will hit the wall and stomp off somewhere. In such instances, he does obey the mother. The mother sees the subject as being age 20 going on 14.

In sixth grade, the subject was forging notes from his teacher to his mother. It seems that the subject can feel that things are not real if he can keep them from his mother. Even with the present charges against him, the subject seems bewildered about the situation. When he would call her from the jail, he would say that he could not stand being himself. He would say that he wanted to crawl out from within his skin.

Soon after getting out on bond and coming home from jail, the subject threw himself on his mother's lap and sobbed. That was the last time the mother saw any emotion expressed by the subject. After that, when she would ask him his feeling about the situation, he would say that he could not think about it or he would collapse. He seems to put things out of his mind so that he can go on functioning. The mother feels that the subject must have been running away from his feelings for years.

The mother feels that the subject began to wall off painful emotions at age 7, when his grandmother died. The subject seemed devastated at the death of the grandmother. At that time, the subject's second-grade teacher commented to the mother that the subject's emotional response to the grandmother's death was inappropriate.

The subject was over his head at Edmonds School. That school fosters and expects independent learning from the students. The subject could not function independently, however. His assignment notebook was filled with doodles and artwork, not a list of homework assignments. If he did his homework, he would lose it before he got it back to school.

If a large assignment was given, such as a project to be handed in a week later, the subject could not break the project down in to workable pieces. The assignment would just be beyond his capability.

Rush School is a school for learning disabled students. The subject's friends there were other troubled children. His girlfriend there was Roxane. She had a wide range of emotions that the subject does not experience. She was very pretty, very spontaneous, and very provocative, but not necessarily sexually provocative. She always had a smart response that would irritate adults.

The subject sees the world as a dangerous place. He saw Roxane as a person who was less secure than himself. He had finally found a person whom he could "take care of." Roxane came from a wealthy middle eastern family that communicated only in explosive verbal interchanges. She was very rebellious.

When the subject would wait in Atlanta for a bus home from school, he hung out with a group of street people in the bus station. He was influenced by these street people. He would cut on himself at times, as evidence of his being troubled. The street people encouraged him to do this. He was afraid that his parents would commit him to a mental hospital, so he ran away, twice. He listened to the street people's indifference to his mother. Once when he ran away, the mother finally had to threaten to no longer be available to the subject, unless he would meet with her. Only with this threat would he would agree to meet with her.

In one runaway incident, Roxane ran away, and the subject ran after her to bring her back. They were both away for about five days. When the mother finally picked them up at a meeting point, the subject had a green mohawk haircut and Roxane had a shaved head with purple bangs. Roxane loved to shock people and do bizarre things. The subject hated to be provocative.

The subject was interested in survival and paramilitary matters starting in about eighth grade. It stemmed from his worry about the world being a dangerous place. His art work portrayed himself as being a big omnipotent monster, and similar themes. The military influence came from the subject's grandfather, who was a well decorated career marine, and the subject's uncle, who was also a career marine. Finally, a neighbor had given the subject a military magazine, from which he sent in coupons. Then the subject began getting loads of paramilitary publications and mailings from the National Rifle Association.

Later, the subject's interest in the paramilitary faded as his obsession with the Beatles increased.

In a recent trip to Italy with an art history class from the Community College, in summer, 1997, the subject did not function as well as the other students. Upon his return, he resumed his psychotherapy. That is when the paramilitary and survival interest resumed.

Once when the subject ran away, he refused to come home unless Roxane came along. Thus, she moved into the subject's house. She was living in the guest room. Roxane disliked being treated as a family member instead of a princess. After 12 days, Roxane chose to return to her father's house.

A few days after Roxane's departure, the subject was taunted, due to his green hair, by others. This was particularly bothersome one time when the family went to the Baskin-Robbins ice cream store for an evening snack. This made the subject angry and made him feel again that the world is unsafe and dangerous. After that, a counselor recommended that the subject see Dr. Kimberly Kandu, an Atlanta Psychiatrist. The subject was then hospitalized at Middleton Psychiatric Hospital in Atlanta.

At Middleton Hospital, the subject was visited by Roxane. However, she would sometimes be blocked from visiting due to her inappropriate clothing. The subject wanted the mother to visit as often as she could.

The subject has always been immature in relation to the mother. At age 14, he would hold her hand as they walked down the street. At this point, he has regressed to calling her Mommy. Last month, a retired physician who met the subject thought that the subject was age 14 or 15.

In twelfth grade, at Jefferson High School in Atlanta, the subject took English, Government, and three art classes. He graduated in June, 1996. He did some amazing art work that year. He seems to function better when he is doing a lot of art work. His art is intensely emotional.

At City Center Community College, the subject's art classes were much more proscribed. He was instructed, for example, to produce a piece of art that shows the use of color. He did not do as well in those art classes.

The subject missed a semester of school after high school graduation. He never did apply to college, so he was not accepted into the community college immediately following high school. He began Community College in January, 1997.

In winter semester, 1997, at Community College, the subject dropped some of his courses, but never told his parents. They did not find out about it until he was in Italy that summer.

The mother felt that the subject was too immature at age 16 to drive a car. The subject did not get a driver's license until age 18.

In autumn, 1996, the subject, with his father's help, signed up for the marines. The subject failed his physical exam, however. The mother was out of town at the time and knew nothing about it. Jack also applied, but was not accepted because he did not have a high school diploma. The subject signed up just because Jack signed up.

The mother does not know how the subject got hooked up with Jack and Sam. She thinks he met Jack through a common friend named Martin Moore. Jack then introduced the subject to Sam.

The subject would let his parents meet his friends, unless they were clearly undesirable characters, such as Martin. The subject let his mother meet Jack and Sam, which indicates that the subject did not know how undesirable Jack and Sam were.

The mother never saw any of the military or survival supplies that the subject purchased in the last year. They were apparently stored at the house were Jack was living. The mother would regularly check the subject's car, because the subject was a pack rat and the car would be messy. She never found any military supplies.

The mother would take the car keys away from the subject when he would come home late with the car. He would be deprived of the car for one or two weeks at a time. She had no suspicions, however, that he was doing anything other than going to movies or similar activities with the car.

Long ago, the mother found some empty beer bottles in the garage, which she suspected were the subject's. In another incident long ago, she found what looked like marijuana residue in his desk. Each time, she confronted him and discussed with him his risk of substance abuse and alcoholism relative to his father being a recovering alcoholic and former substance abuser.

The subject has had no girlfriend since Roxane. He has never had a regular date with a girl. The mother knows of no homosexual experience on the part of the subject.

The subject is impulsive. He never thinks anything through before he does it. If asked why he did something, he never has an explanation.

The subject did not accomplish routine developmental tasks, such as dressing himself, tying his shoes, or using the bathroom independently, until his younger sister accomplished those tasks.

The subject has always seemed to do odd things and behave in odd ways in order to attract the attention of others. However, he has told his mother that he finds it painful to be odd.

When he behaves in a way that is intended to get a response from the mother, he does not seem to care whether the response is negative, positive, or any particular quality. He seems to prefer a more extreme response, regardless of the quality of the response.

As a toddler, when the mother would take the subject to the grocery store, he would talk with her about which loaf of bread to buy, and about everything. He seemed to need the constant stimulation of the verbal interchange. At times, the mother would finally put him in front of the television just to have some time without his talking to her. The subject never seemed to be overstimulated or tired. He always stimulated others to respond to him.

MEDICAL HISTORY

The following is the medical history of this subject, in addition to the above, as told to me by the subject.

The subject's general doctor is Norton Nichols, M.D. The subject was last seen by Dr. Nichols about two months ago when he had a bad cold. Today, the subject is physically healthy.

The subject had a tonsillectomy at about age 3. He has had no other surgeries. The subject has no serious physical illnesses, such as cancer, heart disease, epilepsy, or diabetes.

The subject quit smoking about a week ago. Until that point, he had been smoking up to two packs of cigarettes per day since age 14. In a typical week, the subject's alcohol consumption was about one beer per day and excessive drinking each Tuesday and Thursday. On those days, he started drinking at noon with Sam. Then he would drink in the evening with Jack. He has not had a drink of alcohol, however, since the day of the shooting.

The last time the subject used marijuana was the night of the shooting. Until that point, he would typically smoke marijuana on Tuesdays and Thursdays, both during the day at school and at night with Sam and Jesse.

The pattern of drinking alcohol and smoking marijuana each Tuesday and Thursday began at the beginning of Autumn, 1996. The pattern is predicated on two days off work, Tuesdays and Thursdays. In summer, 1996, he would hang out at Riverside Park in Atlanta and use alcohol and marijuana whenever he was not working. He began smoking marijuana at about age 14. He began drinking alcohol at about age 17.

The subject has used amphetamines, LSD, cocaine, or nitrous oxide at times also. Friends had tanks of nitrous oxide. He has never used any street drug by injection. He has used these substances "because they were there." He used them because the other people present were using them. He used them, he thinks, to fit in with the other people. "They would hand it to me and I would smoke it without thinking about it." He would use one of these substances approximately once a month. The last time he used any of these street drugs, other than alcohol and marijuana, was August, 1996. The subject does not know whether amphetamine psychosis, LSD flashback, or cocaine withdrawal played any part in the shooting.

The subject presently takes no medications. He is supposed to be taking Zoloft, about 10 mg twice a day, prescribed by Dr. Kandu. The subject has been forgetting to take it, and he has not seen Dr. Kandu in a while. The subject last took his Zoloft about three weeks ago.

PSYCHIATRIC HISTORY

The following is the history of the psychiatric aspects of this case, as told to me by the subject.

The subject is treated by Kimberly Kandu, M.D., an Atlanta child psychiatrist. The subject was last seen by her the day after the subject got out of jail, about November 12, 1997. The subject has not seen Dr. Kandu since then because you, his defense attorney, told the subject to avoid discussing his case with anyone.

The subject has been a patient of Dr. Kandu since his admission to Middleton Hospital in December, 1995. The subject did not see Dr. Kandu from about January, 1997, to summer, 1997, because the subject thought that everything was going well. The reason for resuming his treatment in summer, 1997, was his behavior regarding school. He signed up for school and paid for the classes, but he would then fail to attend classes. The subject did not feel good. He wanted to resume his medication. What the subject really wanted in summer, 1997, and still would like today, is to return to Middleton Hospital.

The subject's treatment by Dr. Kandu consisted of medication management and discussion of the subject's relationship with his family. They never talked about the subject's friends or substance abuse. The subject told Dr. Kandu that he had a rifle, but that it was for target practice and hunting.

The medication prescribed by Dr. Kandu helped. It made the subject's behavior better. "I didn't hang out with Jack when I was on the medication."

When the subject was discharged from Middleton Hospital in January, 1996, he did not want to be discharged. He would rather have stayed there because, "It was comfortable and I was making big steps forward." About three weeks after the discharge, his emotional state started to decline again. It declined back to its condition prior to the Middleton admission.

The subject's condition prior to the Middleton admission was, "Probably suicidal and probably very angry all the time." He would pick fights and do things to make others angry at him so that he could be angry at them.

The subject does not know the things at which he was angry. He thinks he was angry at his moving from St. Louis to Atlanta. He did not direct his anger at his parents for the move. He directed the anger at classmates in St. Louis or others. Others in school were scared that the subject would go nuts. Thus, when he would stare them down, they would quiet down and sit on their hands. The subject would dress all in black in eleventh grade, and even wore black fingernail polish. He wore make-up to make is eye sockets look very deep. The subject kept a very scary look on his face, like Charles Manson.

The subject dressed and acted in this way because, "I didn't feel scared if the other people were scared." Looking scary made the subject feel secure. "No one was going to attack me if they were afraid of what I might do." He does not act this way now.

In the summer of 1995, the subject was carving things in his arms with a razor blade. He does not know if he was really suicidal. He does not know why he was cutting himself.

The reasons for his Middleton Hospital admission were the self-mutilation with the razor blades, a recommendation from an education specialist in Atlanta, and the incident at the Baskin Robbins Ice Cream store. The subject, with his green hair and black clothes, was being taunted by others. The subject responded with his scary facial expression. After his mother and his sister took him home from the store, he agreed to go to Middleton Hospital.

The subject was treated in Middleton Hospital by Kandu. The subject's treatment there went pretty smoothly. The subject was a lot more calm while in the hospital. (I asked the subject in many ways what was accomplished, or what changed, during his hospitalization. In response to my questions, he described the friends he had there, the activities the patients did there, and who visited him. He did not describe the therapy, medical treatments, or their effects.) While in the hospital, he didn't hate everything.

While in Middleton, he wanted to go home. But, when the time came for discharge, he did not want to go home.

After the discharge from Middleton, the subject started dressing more normally.

The subject has a learning disability. He cannot understand nonverbal communication or sarcasm. For example, if the tone of a person's voice indicates that the person was being sarcastic, the subject would listen to the words and take them seriously.

The subject is a good reader, but his reading comprehension is poor. He is poor at math computation, even though he understands the theory of math. He is able to do basic addition and subtraction and simple multiplication, but he cannot do any decimal or fraction calculations. He also has short-term memory problems. The subject does not remember the other learning disabilities he has.

At this point, the subject does well in school if he tries really hard. He does better in history, art, and English than in math or science. In eleventh grade, his behavior interfered with his academic performance. He smoked in gym class and got suspended for fighting.

The subject was seen by many psychiatrists prior to Dr. Kandu. He was previously treated by Dr. Thompson in St. Louis, Susan Simpson in St. Louis (now deceased), and several others whose names he cannot remember.

The subject was seen twice by Oscar Olsten, M.D., an Atlanta child psychiatrist, in 1995.

The subject has never been seen by any psychiatrist, psychologist, social worker, or counselor of any sort, other than the above, after Middleton. He was also seen by the Rush High School counselor. He was also seen by the counselor at the Edmonds School.

With regard to sleep, the subject sleeps poorly at this point. He is either too warm or too cold when he tries to sleep. Also he cannot stop thinking about his current situation. For example, it took him 2½ hours to fall asleep last night. He awakened a few times during the night. He slept until his mother awakened him. He slept fine in summer, 1997, although his hours were strange. He slept about 4:00 a.m. to noon.

With regard to appetite, the subject forces himself to eat. In summer, 1997, he ate a lot of snack foods while working in the convenience store.

With regard to memory functioning and concentration ability, the subject has always had a poor short-term memory. His long-term memory is good. He does not remember things very clearly starting in about tenth grade. He also has times from his past he does not remember, for example, the time around his grandfather's death.

The subject has never been able to concentrate well. The only subject on which he is able to concentrate at this point is his legal problems. He tries hard to avoid thinking about his current legal problems because, if he thought about it, he would fall apart. Falling apart means he would cry. He has not cried much since age 8. The last time he cried was the day he got home from jail. "I'm pretty mad at myself for this. One of those bullets could have hit him."

With regard to depressed mood, the subject feels depressed if he thinks about the shooting. He distracts himself with television, computer games, music, household chores, playing with his dogs, or doing art work.

At this point, the subject's usual daily activities consist of staying home and doing his distracting activities. He leaves home only with his mother. He is out of jail on bond, awaiting his trial.

With regard to loss of interest in hobbies and usual activities, the subject has regained his interest in his art work since the shooting. He feels better when he does his art work. He had not done art work for about a year due to frustration. He dislikes taking classes in art. He was frustrated by an art class he was taking at the Atlanta City Center Community College.

The subject denies any recent suicidal thoughts. He last had suicidal thoughts about a week ago. His thought was that, if he ended up going to jail or prison he would have to commit suicide. He also feels, however, that it would be easy to dissuade himself from committing suicide because his mother, father, and sister all love him, and he loves them. He denies any history of suicide attempts. If the subject were to attempt suicide today, the method he would use would be, "Um, boy, I haven't ever. Sometimes I get far enough to think about how I would do it. It would have to end up being sleeping pills, because I wouldn't want to deal with the hurt."

The subject thinks in words, and feels that his thoughts are not hallucinations. He sees a lot of color detail that isn't there. For example, he sees blue, orange, and other colors that others don't see when he looks at a green leaf. He denies any other history of symptoms of hallucinations or delusions. (The subject is not describing symptoms of hallucinations or delusions.)

With regard to loss of energy, the subject feels as if his batteries are dead.

With regard to feelings of worthlessness, the subject no longer feels worthless. He last felt worthless when he got arrested. He feels pretty guilty for putting his parents and the victim through this ordeal. The subject does not feel guilty about Jack or Sam.

With regard to slowed movements, the subject denies feeling as if time is moving in slow motion. He feels as if time is moving quickly.

The subject denies the symptoms of mania. He denies manic sleep pattern. He sometimes talks fast. He buys a lot of computer games, books, and music disks. He denies grandiose plans. (The subject is not describing mania.)

In general, the subject would describe himself, presently, as a person who is, "I'm not sure. I think remorseful. Um. I think I'm a little different than I was. Certainly my mind set is a little different. I think I'm a little more wary about who I'm going to choose as friends."

In general, the subject would describe himself as a person who was, about six months ago, "Hateful, irrational, eccentric, irresponsible, incoherent."

HISTORY OF LEGAL ASPECTS OF THIS CASE

The following are the legal aspects of this case, as told to me by the subject.

The subject has never been in legal difficulties other than the current charges against him. He will never be in legal trouble again in the future. He is willing to be on probation forever, or do as much community service as it takes to avoid jail.

The subject presently is not self-supporting. He is living at home with his parents. His previous employer, Cathy's Convenience Store, has offered him his job back when his legal problems are resolved.

The subject has never been sued by any party. He has never sued any party. He has never been in jail prior to the arrest for the shooting.

PERSONAL AND FAMILY HISTORY

The following is the personal and family history of this subject, as told to me by the subject.

The subject was born on July 1, 1978, in St. Louis, Missouri. At age 17, he moved to Atlanta because his father was transferred here. He is now age 20.

The subject's mother is age 42 and healthy. She is not presently employed. She used to be employed as a registered nurse. She does volunteer work for about 10 different charities, which keeps her busy. The subject is close to her.

The subject's father is age 42. He works as a computer consultant for the ABC Computer Company. The subject is not really close to him. They get along okay. The subject gets mad at him a lot for failing to take the subject's, or anyone else's needs, into consideration. He is not a considerate person. He is moody and gets mad at everyone at least once a week for a few days. He often gets mad at the subject or the subject's mother, but never gets mad at

George Gunner
January 1, 1999
page 31

the subject's sister. Once, at age 9, the subject hit his mother in the arm because he was mad at her. The father told him that, if he ever hit his mother again, he would break the subject's arms.

The father hit the subject only once, when the subject was age 12. The subject is often mad at the father, usually about six days per week. The father is domineering. The subject and his father do get along with each other, even though the subject is angry at him most of the time.

The father has a history of both alcoholism and substance abuse. He has been abstinent from both for the last six years.

This is the first marriage for both parents. They have been married 22 years.

The subject has only one sibling, a sister age 17. The subject is very close to her. She is a junior at Thomas Jefferson High School in Atlanta.

The subject has never been married and has no children.

With regard to whether religion plays an important part in this subject's life: "Not until recently, when they moved me from Unit D up to Unit H in the jail." One of his two Puerto Rican cellmates handed the subject a Bible. At that point, religion became important to the subject. As a baby, he was baptized Catholic. At about age 14, he abandoned everything that was important to his parents, including religion, and made up his own values. Today, his values are once again the same as his parents' values.

One thing the subject would like to do in the future is talk to the victim, Mr. Ingham, and compassionately tell him that he is sorry for all of this. "I honestly feel bad for what has happened and would like to do my best to rectify the situation. I don't feel that I really ever hated people for their race, creed, or religion, or whatever." The subject feels that he can best rectify the situation by changing the rest of his life.

The subject now finds that he likes dressing in normal clothes. He likes the idea of liking other people, and being liked by them, and getting along with them.

George Gunner
January 1, 1999
page 32

MENTAL STATUS EXAMINATION

The following are the answers given by the subject to my asking him mental status examination questions.

The date is, "December 31, 1998." I am, "Dr. Berger." This room is, "It's an office." The presidents in reverse order are, "Bill Clinton, George Bush, Ronald Reagan, Jimmy Carter." Serially subtracting $7 from $100, "93, 86, 79, 72, 65."

If the subject were walking down the street and found a letter lying next to a mailbox, he would, "Put it in the mailbox." If the subject were in a theater and saw the curtains on fire, he would, "Yell FIRE." If someone said to the subject that the grass is always greener on the other side of the fence, that person would be trying to say, "See, this is one of the things I had trouble with in my educational testing. Things that we don't have look better than the things we do have." If someone said, don't cry over spilled milk, that would mean, "Don't worry about things you can't change." The subject has difficulty putting into words what proverbs mean. He can use the proverbs correctly, but cannot easily interpret them into words. The subject's inability to put abstract thoughts into words is not as bad as it used to be.

I observe the subject to be oriented to person, place, and time. His attitude is cooperative. He is obviously immature. An observer would assume that he is about age 14 due to his speech pattern and speech content. His appearance and mannerisms are that of a 16-year-old. He is indecisive in his actions. He waited for me to indicate that he should follow me from the waiting room into my office. He looked at his mother before doing so. He did not walk with me until his mother nodded to him to do so.

In my examining room, he did not look around or make a motion to sit down until I invited him to have a seat on the couch. He then did so without hesitation. He sat smiling pleasantly, and silently, until I sat down and looked at him, then he started asking me small talk type questions. He asked if that was a picture of my family on my desk. He commented that I have a lot of diplomas on the wall and a lot of books on the shelves. He asked the subjects of the books, etc.

The subject's thought content lacks depth. He does not appear to think about his answers to questions, his situation, or his own feelings. He seems to have no feelings or thoughts of his own. He seems to only regurgitate the thoughts and feelings that others have told him he should have. During my examination of him, he appeared to be looking for cues from me as to how he should respond to my questions. When I cued him, he followed my cues, even when my cues were obviously incorrect. For example, when he correctly told me that the date is December 31, 1998, I responded with a questioning facial expression. He then responded by asking me if it was really December 30, the day before New Year's Eve. I then did not respond. I instead looked down at my computer. He then said, "That's right. It's December 30. Tomorrow is New Years' Eve."

When I asked the subject an abstract question of values, such as whether it was right for his cellmate to give him a Bible, he hemmed and hawed, and replied with neutral statements, such as, "He gave it to me." With no feedback or cuing from me, the subject never did answer whether it was right or wrong. When I said, "Well, you were baptized as a baby, weren't you," then the subject said that it was right for the cellmate to give him the Bible.

The subject's affect is not depressed, angry, or anxious. His affect is not happy or sad. He smiles as if he has no cares in the world and no thoughts in his head. He appears to have no feelings, good or bad. His affect seems empty.

The subject is able to laugh and smile. These are appropriate to the context of the conversation. They seem rehearsed rather than genuine. They also follow my cues. If he started to laugh at something, he looked at me before continuing to laugh. If I was laughing, he would continue to laugh. If I was not laughing, he would stop laughing and sit quietly until I said something, or until about

20 seconds of silence occurred. After a silence, he would then ramble about some topic loosely connected to the last sentence. For example, if the last sentence was about a television program, he would the end the silence by telling me about a music CD that he recently bought.

The subject lacks insight. He manifests no indication of having any values that are his own, or even any thoughts that are his own.

The subject's speech pattern is singsong, as if he is a child repeating nursery rhymes. He does have inflection in his voice, but it seems to be unconnected to any feeling or thoughts behind his words. His inflections seem rehearsed.

The subject appears to make no judgments. He appears to select whatever value or judgment I indicate verbally or nonverbally.

The subject exhibits no indication of psychotic thought disorder. The subject appears to have subnormal intelligence, but he does not appear to be mentally retarded.

PSYCHOLOGICAL TESTS

As you requested, psychological testing has not yet been arranged. If you would like me to have formal psychological testing done, I will do so. IQ and MMPI testing would be helpful in validating the findings of my examination of the subject. It is my impression that the subject's IQ is about 90. It is my judgment that he does not qualify for a diagnosis of mental retardation.

OBJECTIVE OBSERVATIONS

The following are my objective observations regarding this subject.

The subject was present on schedule for his psychiatric examination appointment. He was appropriately groomed with normal brown hair, about two inches long. He was appropriately dressed in a yellow knit shirt, blue jeans, jogger shoes, and blue sox. He had no earrings or jewelry of any sort. His fingernails had no polish. He is clean-shaven. The general appearance of this subject is that of a normal 16-year-old young man.

The subject appeared to be interested in staying out of jail or prison. He also seemed interested in apologizing to Mr. Ingham. Otherwise, he seemed interesting in giving me answers that would please me. In my examination of the subject, he appeared to have no motivations other than these.

The subject exhibits no apparent movement disorders, gait disturbances, or general physical discomforts.

My examination of the subject began at 9:00 a.m. and ended at 12:34 p.m. on December 31, 1998. My appointment with his mother began at 2:30 p.m. and ended at 5:14 p.m. on December 31, 1998.

PSYCHODYNAMIC FORMULATION

The following is my psychodynamic formulation, my psychiatric explanation, of how the subject's mind works.

The subject has no thoughts of his own. His mind does not have any values, thoughts, preferences, or ordering of ideas. He simply lacks the usual feelings and thoughts that normal people have.

The subject has gotten through life so far by (1) following the path of least resistance and (2) taking cues from others. Following the path of least resistance occurs when, for example, the subject is sent to his room as a punishment and he ends up listening to his CD player, having forgotten why he is in his room. Taking cues from others occurs as described in the text of the above report in the Mental Status section. The subject initiates no action or response until he is cued by another person.

In essence, the subject has no thoughts and no motivations. His thoughts are random and lacking direction. He does as he is told or cued. He does not initiate any actions on his own.

George Gunner
January 1, 1999
page 36

CONCLUSIONS

The following are my answers to your questions, as an independent forensic psychiatric examiner.

1. What is the psychiatric diagnosis of this subject?

Axis I: None
Axis II: Personality disorder NOS 301.9
Axis III: None
Axis IV: Pending criminal charges
Axis V: Current: 70
            In the last year: 70

This diagnosis in this subject is characterized by having no thoughts or feelings of his own and making no decisions on his own during his entire life. He only reflects the instructions, teachings, and cues he receives from others.

2. Is the subject incompetent to stand trial?

In Georgia, a person is competent to stand trial if the person has sufficient present ability to consult with his lawyer with a reasonable degree of rational understanding, and whether he has a rational, as well as factual, understanding of the proceedings against him.

This subject is able to cooperate with his attorney in his own defense. He has sufficient present ability to consult with his attorney with a reasonable degree of rational understanding. He is able, with a reasonable degree of rational understanding, to weigh the pros and cons of any options available to him. However, he is unable to make decisions on his own about the best option for his circumstances. He is able to rely on the advice and guidance of others for making such decisions, including his attorney.

The subject has a rational understanding of the proceedings against him. He comprehends the charges and the possible consequences. He is able to describe them without prompting.

George Gunner
January 1, 1999
page 37

The subject has a factual understanding of the proceedings against him. He is able to accurately state the charges without prompting. He is also able to describe the events of November 1, 1997, that have led to these charges.

3. Does the subject fulfill the criteria for legal insanity regarding the charges of (a) attempted murder, (b) unlawful possession of a firearm, and (c) conspiracy to commit murder regarding the events of November 1, 1997?

In Georgia, a person is criminally responsible if, as a result of mental illness, that person lacks substantial capacity to (1) appreciate the nature and quality, or wrongfulness, of his acts, or (2) conform his conduct to the requirements of the law.

A.   Regarding the charge of attempted murder:

(1)   This subject has a mental illness, personality disorder NOS 301.9, as described above.
(2)   As a result of his mental illness, the subject did not lack substantial capacity to understand the nature and quality, or wrongfulness, of his actions. He states that he intentionally shot the gun in a direction such that the bullets would miss Mr. Ingham. This shows that the subject knew that shooting Mr. Ingham would be harmful to Mr. Ingham, and was wrong.

However, with regard to intent, the subject felt that he was not attempting murder. The subject feels that he was only following orders, and following them in a way that would avoid anyone getting hurt. He was following the order to shoot at Mr. Ingham by shooting in the direction of Mr. Ingham. But his intent was to avoid harming anyone. He was avoiding harm to Mr. Ingham by aiming such that the bullets would miss Mr. Ingham. As it turned out, one of the bullets somehow grazed Mr. Ingham anyway. The subject was avoiding harm to himself by shooting when ordered to shoot.

George Gunner
January 1, 1999
page 38

The subject believed that he would be killed if he failed to follow Jack's orders. The subject's following the orders, but in a way that would avoid harm to anyone, shows that he knew that attempting to murder Mr. Ingham was wrong.

(3) As a result of his mental illness, the subject was not able to conform his conduct to the requirements of the law. As described in the text of the above report, the subject is not able to control his behavior in any setting, including the shooting incident on November 1, 1997. He follows the cues of others or he behaves in a simply random, directionless path of least resistance without any thinking involved. He does not select which behaviors he pursues. He simply follows directions, like water flowing to the lowest level without making any decision about which way to flow. In the shooting incident, he was simply following Jack's orders without any thought or self-control.

B. Regarding the charge of unlawful possession of a firearm:

(1) This subject has a mental illness, personality disorder NOS 301.9, as described above.

(2) As a result of his mental illness, the subject did not lack substantial capacity to understand the nature and quality, or wrongfulness, of unlawfully possessing a firearm. The subject did know that he owned an unregistered gun. He also knew that the gun Jack handed him, the gun with which he shot in the direction of Mr. Ingham, was unregistered. He knew that possessing an unregistered gun was unlawful.

(3) As a result of his mental illness, the subject was not able to conform his conduct to the requirements of the law. As described in the text of the above report, the subject is not able to control his behavior in any setting. He follows the cues and instructions of others or he behaves in a simply random, directionless path of least resistance without any thinking

involved. He does not select which behaviors he pursues. He simply follows directions, like water flowing to the lowest level without making any decision about which way to flow. When Jack told the subject to buy a gun without registering it, he did it because he was told to do so. When Jack ordered the subject to take Jack's gun and shoot at Mr. Ingham, he did it because he was ordered to do so.

C. Regarding the charge of conspiracy to commit murder:

(1) This subject has a mental illness, personality disorder NOS 301.9, as described above.

(2) As a result of his mental illness, the subject did not lack substantial capacity to understand the nature and quality, or wrongfulness, of conspiring to commit murder. The subject knew that conspiring to commit murder was wrong.

However, with regard to intent, the subject felt that he was not conspiring to commit murder. The subject feels that he was only following orders, but following them in a way that would avoid anyone getting hurt. He was following Jack's order to shoot at Mr. Ingham by shooting in the direction of Mr. Ingham. But his intent was to avoid harming anyone. He was avoiding harm to Mr. Ingham by aiming such that the bullets would miss Mr. Ingham. As it turned out, one of the bullets somehow grazed Mr. Ingham anyway. The subject was avoiding harm to himself by shooting when ordered by Jack to shoot. The subject believed that he would be killed if he failed to follow Jack's orders.

(3) As a result of his mental illness, the subject was not able to conform his conduct to the requirements of the law. As described in the text of the above report, the subject is not able to control his behavior in any setting. He follows the cues and instructions of others or he behaves in a simply random, directionless path of least resistance without any thinking

involved. He does not select which behaviors he pursues. He simply follows directions, like water flowing to the lowest level without making any decision about which way to flow. When he shot the gun in the direction of Mr. Ingham, the subject was simply doing as he was told to do by Jack, and was simultaneously doing as he had been taught during his upbringing, to not hurt anyone.

If you have any further questions, please let me know; also, if I can clarify any issues for you, I will be happy to do so.

I appreciate the opportunity to examine this interesting young man.

I do give you my consent to release this report to any appropriate party.

Sincerely yours,

Steven H. Berger, M.D.
Diplomate, American Board of Psychiatry and Neurology
Diplomate, American Board of Forensic Psychiatry

WORKERS' COMPENSATION DEFENSE CASE:
DELORES DEPRESSED

STEVEN H. BERGER, M.D.
Psychiatric Consultation Services

1234 Parchment Drive, SE   Detroit, Michigan 12345-6789
Office phone: 616-957-0850   fax: 616-957-3045
Home phone: 616-949-6734   E-mail: SHBergerMD@aol.com

December 31, 1999

American Evaluations, Inc.
Greenfield Building
12345 Greenfield Road, Suite 678
Detroit, Michigan 12345-6789

Re: Mrs. Delores Depressed

Dear Sir:

At your request, I performed a psychiatric independent medical evaluation (IME) of Mrs. Delores Depressed in my office on December 31, 1999. The purpose of this IME is to answer your questions regarding this subject's ability to perform work duties. These questions are detailed at the end of this report.

At the beginning of my examination, I explained to the subject the purpose of this examination, that my findings would not be confidential, and that I would be sending my report to you. Understanding all of those explanations, she agreed to proceed with the examination.

The following are my findings and conclusions regarding that evaluation.

The following is the history given to me by the subject.

The subject is age 46. She is employed by the City of Detroit. Her position is parole officer for the Detroit Recorders Court. She works in the Griffin Building in downtown Detroit. She last

Delores Depressed
December 31, 1999
page 2

worked at that employment on June 28, l999. The reason she did not return to work after that date was because, "Ah, depression."

The psychiatrist treating the subject is, "Joy Jones and Barry Barton." (Joy Jones is a limited licensed psychologist. Barry Barton is a Ph.D. psychologist.) The office of these two people is on Alger Street in Detroit. The subject was last seen by Jones last week. The subject was last seen by Barton last month.

The subject takes no psychiatric medications. She takes other medications, but she does not remember the name of them. (Later, the subject was able to find in her purse a list of the medications she takes.) The medications the subject takes are nortriptyline, 1 tablet per day at bedtime; asthma medications as needed, and Fiorinal as needed for migraine headaches. The nortriptyline is prescribed by Dr. Smith in Texas. The Fiorinal is prescribed by Dr. Humbolt in Detroit.

With regard to symptoms, the subject sleeps poorly due to her fibromyalgia. With regard to appetite, she eats all the time. She is unable to concentrate. She does feel depressed. She wants to sleep all the time. She cries all the time. The subject has lost interest in sex, grooming, and housekeeping.

With regard to suicidal thoughts, the subject wants to wake up dead. She does not want to kill herself. She denies any history of suicide attempts.

The subject denies the symptoms of psychosis.

The subject lacks energy. She feels like a failure. She denies feeling slowed down.

The subject denies inappropriate euphoria, manic sleep pattern, manic speech pattern, manic spending pattern, or grandiosity.

The subject denies the use of alcohol, street drugs, cigarettes, or caffeine.

With regard to her physical health, the subject has fibromyalgia, a bulging disc in her lower back, knee problems that cause her to limp and be unable to walk steps, chronic pain, and pain in her

Delores Depressed
December 31, 1999
page 3

hip, knee, and right hand. She also has asthma. She had breast cancer two years ago and is still going through reconstructive surgeries for that.

The subject lives with her husband. She has two children. One
child is away at college. The other child is in tenth grade and lives
at home.

The subject was scheduled to return to work on September 30,
1999. However, Joy Jones extended that date to an undesignated
time. The subject feels that she is unable to do her job at this point.
She is unable to do her job because she cannot concentrate and she
cannot fulfill the physical demands of her work.

At this point, the subject spends her time, "I really don't do anything." She sometimes prepares meals, cleans her house, does her
laundry, or bathes. She occasionally goes to church, watches television, or reads. She does not visit friends. She does not go grocery
shopping.

The following are my observations regarding this subject.

The subject is alert, oriented, and appropriate. She does cry easily. She did cry during her time with me. She did not smile or
laugh during her time with me.

The patient is calm and cooperative. She is friendly. There is no
sign of psychotic thought disorder. Although she admits that she
prefers to be dead, she denies suicidal ideation.

The patient's affect is depressed. She appears to be sad over her
physical limitations. She also cried when she talked about the
shortage of money that she and her husband have.

The following are my answers to your questions, based upon
the above history and findings, as an independent psychiatric
forensic examiner.

1. What is the subject's current disability medical history? The
    subject's current disability medical history is detailed in the
    text of the above report.

Delores Depressed
December 31, 1999
page 4

2. What is the subject's past medical history? The subject's past medical history is detailed in the text of the above report.

3. What are the subjective complaints of the subject? The subjective complaints of the subject are detailed in the text of the above report.

4. What are your clinical objective findings regarding this subject? My clinical objective findings regarding this subject are detailed in the text of the above report.

5. What is the current psychiatric diagnosis of this subject? The current psychiatric diagnosis of this subject is major depressive disorder, 296.22. This diagnosis in this subject is characterized by sleep disturbance, appetite disturbance, poor concentration ability, depressed mood, loss of interest in her usual activities, feeling that she would prefer to be dead, lack of energy, and feeling like a failure.

6. What is the prognosis for this subject's major depressive disorder? The prognosis for this subject's major depressive disorder is fair. If she did not have her physical illnesses, her prognosis for her depressive illness would be good. However, it is her physical illnesses that depress her, and her physical illnesses have a fair to poor prognosis.

7. What are your recommendations regarding treatment for this subject's major depressive illness? I recommend that this subject be treated by a psychiatrist for her major depressive disorder. Her medication program for her major depressive disorder appears to be inadequate. From the information available to me, I am unable to determine whether the psychotherapy treatment being rendered by Joy Jones and Barry Barton is appropriate or adequate.

8. Is this subject totally disabled or not totally disabled from her own occupation? This subject is presently totally disabled from her own occupation.

Delores Depressed
December 31, 1999
page 5

9. What are the present mental limitations, mental restrictions, and mental capabilities of this subject? As described above, the subject has difficulty concentrating, her mood is depressed, she has little enthusiasm or interest, she has little energy, and she has little self esteem. She is capable of doing some simple tasks some of the time.

10. What are the present physical limitations, physical restrictions, and physical capabilities of this subject? The physical limitations, physical restrictions, and physical capabilities of this subject will have to be determined by a physician who physically examines the subject. I did not physically examine her. I performed a psychiatric evaluation.

11. If the subject is presently unable to return to her own occupation, what is your estimate of the duration of her disability? It is my estimate that it will be at least one month, after the subject starts receiving appropriate psychiatric treatment, before she will once again be capable of performing the duties of her own occupation.

12. Is further treatment necessary for this subject in relation to her major depressive disorder? Yes, as described above.

I thank you for the opportunity to examine this interesting case. If I can address any further questions or clarify any issues, I will be happy to do so if you will send your further questions in writing. I do give you my consent to release this report to any appropriate party.

Sincerely,

Steven H. Berger, M.D.
Diplomate, American Board of Psychiatry and Neurology, with Added Qualifications in Forensic Psychiatry

WORKERS' COMPENSATION PLAINTIFF'S CASE:
HENRY HEALTHY

STEVEN H. BERGER, M.D.
Psychiatric Consultation Services

1234 Parchment Drive, SE   Detroit, Michigan 12345-6789
Office phone: 616-957-0850   fax: 616-957-3045
Home phone: 616-949-6734   E-mail: SHBergerMD@aol.com

December 31, 1999

American Evaluations, Inc.
Greenfield Building
12345 Greenfield Road, Suite 678
Detroit, Michigan 12345-6789

Re: Mr. Henry Healthy

Dear Sir:

At your request, I performed a psychiatric independent medical evaluation (IME) of Mr. Henry Healthy in my office on December 31, 1999. The purpose of this evaluation was to determine if the subject, Mr. Healthy, is presently able to perform the duties of his regular employment.

At the beginning of my examination, I explained to the subject the purpose of the examination. I explained that the usual confidentiality that patients expect from physicians does not apply to this examination. I told him that I would be sending my report to you. After this explanation, he agreed to proceed with my examination of him.

The following are my findings and conclusions regarding that evaluation.

The following is the history given to me by the subject.

The subject is age 46. He is employed by the City of Detroit. His position is parole officer for the Detroit Recorders Court. He works in the Griffin Building in downtown Detroit. He last worked at that employment on June 28, 1999. The reason he did not return to work after that date was because, "Depression."

The psychiatrist treating the subject is Robert Regis, M.D., on Alger Street in Detroit. The subject was last seen by Regis last week.

The subject takes no psychiatric medications. He takes Lopressor and Fiorinal. These are prescribed by Dr. Humbolt in Detroit.

With regard to symptoms, the subject sleeps poorly due to his worry over money. With regard to appetite, he is hungry at meal times. He has a difficult time concentrating. He does feel mildly depressed. He cries at times, over his financial situation. The subject denies loss of interest in sex, grooming, or housekeeping.

With regard to suicidal thoughts, the subject denies suicidal thoughts. He denies any history of suicide attempts.

The subject denies the symptoms of psychosis.

The subject lacks energy at times, particularly after a sleepless night. He feels like a failure due to his great amount of debt. He denies feeling slowed down.

The subject denies inappropriate euphoria, manic sleep pattern, manic speech pattern, manic spending pattern, or grandiosity.

The subject denies the use of alcohol, street drugs, cigarettes, or caffeine.

The subject is physically healthy except for high blood pressure.

The subject lives with his wife and one of his two children. One child is away at college.

The subject was scheduled to return to work on September 30, 1999. However, Dr. Regis extended that date to an undesignated time. The subject feels that he is unable to do his job at this point because he cannot concentrate and he cannot fulfill the physical demands of his work. He feels he is too tired all the time to do his work.

At this point, the subject spends his time, "I really don't do anything." He sometimes prepares meals, cleans the house, does his laundry, or showers. He occasionally goes to church, watches television, or reads. He does not visit friends. He does not go grocery shopping.

Henry Healthy
December 31, 1999
page 2

The following are my observations regarding this subject.

The subject is alert, oriented, appropriate, calm, cooperative, likeable, and friendly. He did exhibit appropriate smiling and laughing during his time with me.

The subject exhibits no sign of psychotic thought disorder or suicidal ideation.

The patient's affect is not depressed. He appears to be sad, embarrassed, and angry over his financial situation. He cried when he talked about his shortage of money.

The following is my answer to your question, based upon the above history and findings, as an independent psychiatric forensic examiner.

1. Is this subject presently able to perform the duties of his regular employment?

    Yes. There is no psychiatric finding at this time which renders this subject unable to perform the usual duties of his usual employment as probation officer.

I thank you for the opportunity to examine this interesting case. If I can address any further questions or clarify any issues, I will be happy to do so if you will send them in writing. I do give you my consent to release this report to any appropriate party.

Sincerely,

Steven H. Berger, M.D.
Diplomate, American Board of Psychiatry and Neurology, with Added Qualifications in Forensic Psychiatry

Index

Accreditation Council for Graduate Medical Education (ACGME), 117–18
Added Qualifications certification, 117–18
address, for a written report, 60–61
advance payments, request for, in a service agreement, 32
advertising, 111–15
advocate, forensic psychiatrist as, 22, 104
affidavit, defined, 15
agencies, for litigation experts, 113
American Academy of Child and Adolescent Psychiatry, professional liability insurance sponsorship, 110
American Academy of Psychiatry and the Law (AAPL), 122–23
  access through, to the American Board of Forensic Psychiatry, 118
  ethical principles stated by, 102–4
  review course sponsored by, 119
American Board of Forensic Psychiatry, 118
American College of Forensic Examiners, 118, 123
American College of Forensic Psychiatry, 123
American College of Forensic Sciences, 123
American Medical Association (AMA), 122
  principles of medical ethics, 101–2
American Psychiatric Association (APA), 122
  handling of complaints of unethical conduct, 103–4

principles of medical ethics, 101–2
professional liability insurance sponsorship, 109
Americans with Disabilities Act (ADA), the forensic psychiatrist's evaluation in terms of, 24
anxiety disorder, treating physician's testimony about, 10
aphasia, caretaker presence in examining a person with, 51
appeals court, defined, 15
appointment, for a forensic examination, arranging, 45–46
approaches, to advertising, 112–16
argument, with an opposing attorney, 98
assessment, in a written report, 60
attendees, at a deposition, 83
attorney
  examinee's, presence during an examination, 51
  opposing, disruption of an examination by, 53
  presence of, at a deposition, 83
  strategist role of, 9
  subpoena issued by, 79
  see also retaining attorney
attorney work product
  defined, 15
  discoverability of, 38–39
  information and opinions of an expert witness as, 70–71
  information gathered in an examination as, 47
  notes about records as, 41–42
audiotaping, during an examination, 55